The Critical Idiom
General Editor: JOHN D. JUMP

15 Pastoral

Pastoral / *Peter V. Marinelli*

Methuen & Co Ltd

First published 1971
by Methuen & Co Ltd
11 New Fetter Lane, London, EC4
© 1971 Peter V. Marinelli
Printed in Great Britain
by Cox & Wyman Ltd, Fakenham, Norfolk

SBN 416 08700 0 Hardback
SBN 416 08710 8 Paperback

Distributed in the U.S.A.
by Barnes & Noble Inc.

Contents

General Editor's Preface

This volume is one of a series of short studies, each dealing with a single key item, or a group of two or three key items, in our critical vocabulary. The purpose of the series differs from that served by the standard glossaries of literary terms. Many terms are adequately defined for the needs of students by the brief entries in these glossaries, and such terms will not be the subjects of studies in the present series. But there are other terms which cannot be made familiar by means of compact definitions. Students need to grow accustomed to them through simple and straightforward but reasonably full discussions of them. The purpose of this series is to provide such discussions.

Some of the terms in question refer to literary movements (e.g., 'Romanticism', 'Aestheticism', etc.), others to literary kinds (e.g., 'Comedy', 'Epic', etc.), and still others to stylistic features (e.g., 'Irony', 'The Conceit', etc.). Because of this diversity of subject-matter, no attempt has been made to impose a uniform pattern upon the studies. But all authors have tried to provide as full illustrative quotation as possible, to make reference whenever appropriate to more than one literature, and to compose their studies in such a way as to guide readers towards the short bibliographies in which they have made suggestions for further reading.

John D. Jump

University of Manchester

I

Perspectives on the Pastoral

Towards the beginning of the eighth book of Wordsworth's *The Prelude*, a book entitled 'Retrospect – Love of Nature Leading to Love of Man', there occurs a passage of almost two hundred lines which is of distinct importance to the pastoral tradition. It begins with a notable paragraph on the growth of the poet's love of humanity, a paragraph which terminates in a simple assertion about a class of simple men:

> For me, when my affections first were led
> From kindred, friends, and playmates, to partake
> Love for the human creature's absolute self,
> That noticeable kindliness of heart
> Sprang out of fountains, there abounding most,
> Where sovereign Nature dictated the tasks
> And occupations which her beauty adorned,
> And Shepherds were the men that pleased me first. . . .
>
> (121–8)

The word 'Shepherd', rendered more prominent by the capitalization, is for any reader in the European tradition an evocatory one. But the resonances of the word may move us too suddenly into a wistful recollection of the meadows and pastures of the golden Arcadias of classical pastoral, and therefore Wordsworth is prompt to clarify his meaning. He does so by interposing a series of idyllic reminiscences which lovingly record the development of the earlier pastoral, and at the same time divide it sharply from his own conception of that form of life and of the literature it inspires. He approaches the issue by a series of negative definitions. The Shepherds with whom he is concerned are not those whom Saturn ruled in the Latian wilds and who have left 'even to us toiling in this late day,/A bright tradition of the golden age'. They are not such as 'mid Arcadian fastnesses' made a tradition of 'Felicity, in Grecian song renowned'. They are not such as entered 'with Shakespeare's genius' the forests of Arden or the rustic setting where Perdita and Florizel 'Together danced, Queen of the feast, and King'. Nor, finally (and the concision of the allusion is attributable perhaps to the wealth of pastoral forms to be found in this author), are they 'such as Spenser fabled'. The Shepherd who plays so significant a part in Wordsworth's own spiritual development is rather a type whose rural ways and manners were the 'unluxuriant product of a life/Intent on little but substantial needs. . . .' The line 'Smooth life had flock and shepherd in old time' points the contrast neatly: the fanciful creatures of old pastoral on the one hand, and the actual shepherd of modern times on the other. And though there are points of contact between the two – the latter also 'tunes a flageolet to liquid notes of love', he too occasionally spends hours of 'unlaborious pleasure, with no task/More toilsome than to carve a beechen bowl' – the poet is constantly aware that his contemporaries more usually move under skies less generous and serene than those of the ancient Mediterranean, in landscapes of wintry snows, hard labour, terrifying winds and an overawing solitude. In the poet's idealizing imagination, the actual Shepherd assumes a giant shape: he becomes, beheld single against the sky, 'A solitary object and sublime'. It is, perhaps, because the modern shepherd unites sublimity and reality that Wordsworth can draw the ultimate comparison between the delicate creatures of Arcadian fiction and what is essentially a moral being:

> this creature – spiritual almost
> As those of books, but more exalted far;

Far more of an imaginative form
Than the gay Corin of the groves, who lives
For his own fancies, or to dance by the hour,
In coronal, with Phyllis in the midst —
Was, for the purposes of kind, a man
With the most common; husband, father; learned,
Could teach, admonish; suffered with the rest,
From vice and folly, wretchedness and fear. . . .

(282–91)

The passage from which we have drawn these quotations is a microcosm of the old pastoral genre; a recollection, almost elegiac in tone, of its great age, its immense variety; and a witness of its death in the latter eighteenth century and its rebirth in the nineteenth under quite a different aspect. For if pastoral lives for us at all at the present time, it lives by a capacity to move out of its old haunts in the Arcadian pastures and to inhabit the ordinary country landscapes of the modern world, daily contracted by the encroachment of civilization and as a consequence daily more precious as a projection of our desires for simplicity. In the modern sense, pastoral is a very broad and very general term far removed from the more specific and distinct meaning attributed to it in earlier times. It scarcely has reference to a literature about actual shepherds, much less about Arcadians. For us it has come to mean any literature which deals with the complexities of human life against a background of simplicity. All that is necessary is that memory and imagination should conspire to render a not too distant past of comparative innocence as more pleasurable than a harsh present, overwhelmed either by the growth of technology or the shadows of advancing age. Certain Victorian novels, those of George Eliot for instance, deal with life in country settings in a period anterior to the Industrial Revolution and express the movement from complexity to simplicity in both time and place. In a more modern instance, we have exchanged the soft primitivism of Arcadia for a hard primitivism in New Hampshire and in so doing found it possible to speak of the pastoral part of Robert Frost. Instructed by William Empson we have been taught to see a sociological pastoral in works as diverse at *The Beggar's Opera* and *Alice in Wonderland*. Or we have begun to transfer the aspects of the pastoral golden age into the time of innocence that every individual can remember, and to speak of a pastoral of childhood. Either the machines have come into the garden, or the world of adult experience casts its long shadows: in any case, it is a long time since the shepherds have all departed, leaving no addresses.

In confronting the literary tradition of pastoral then, in opposing to it a world of contemporary or just-outgrown pastoral reality, Wordsworth and some of his immediate predecessors like George Crabbe in effect draw a line, apparently for ever, between the classical and the modern pastoral. Corin and Phyllis, generic names for an entire host of shepherds and shepherdesses of the antique tradition, function only in the world of literature; their dwelling-place is in a golden country of the imagination called Arcadia, and their time is that timeless time of the mind in regression from reality. They are shepherds hardly at all, for their real interests are love and poetry, and they are really only the occasion for poetry. By contrast, the shepherds of Wordsworth are real; they inhabit a familiar landscape of Grasmere Vale and Helvellyn, and they move in the world of the present or at least of the proximate past; they are the subject-matter of poetry. When Wordsworth in 1800 published a poem about realistic though idealized contemporary shepherd life called *Michael* and boldly subtitled it 'A Pastoral Poem', he was in effect challenging an entire conception of pastoral: the day of the courtly Corin was over. Earlier still, in 1783, when George Crabbe in *The Village* complained that 'To sing of shepherds is an easy task', his concern for the harried shepherd forced to beg from 'Nature's niggard hand' led him to open attack upon the conventions of classical pastoral:

I grant indeed that fields and flocks have charms
For him that grazes or for him that farms;
But when amid such pleasing scenes I trace
The poor laborious natives of the place,
And see the midday sun, with fervid ray,
On their bare heads and dewy temples play;
While some, with feebler heads and fainter hearts,
Deplore their fortune, yet sustain their parts,
Then shall I dare these real ills to hide
In tinsel trappings of poetic pride?

(Book I, 39–48)

Even from so brief a consideration of pastoral from the point of view of those for whom and by whom one of its versions, the oldest and most long-lived, was definitely ended, it becomes apparent that the definition of pastoral is no simple matter. In the first place, from the time when Arcadia goes – from the Romantics thenceforward – all pastoral myths are essentially private pastoral myths. In the second place, the change of myth involves a change of attitude. In the universal myth of Arcadia we have a world of leisure, song and love that represents an idealization; in the private myth, what Wordsworth calls the 'dignities of plain occurrence', real though idealized, and interfused, perhaps inseparable from, a strong humanitarian sentiment. Now the emotions of pity and indignation are not only foreign, they are wholly inapplicable to the shepherd of the old pastoral. At first glance, the Arcadians are so comparatively felicitous in their lives and apparently so remote from actuality, that the question of sympathy for their lot never arises. The question is not one of mere heartlessness in our forebears, and a word of explanation upon this point is necessary. In general, classical pastoral begins with a conception of man and of human nature and locates it in a specific type, the shepherd, the simplicity of whose life is the goal towards which all existence strives; of that life, the individual details, the labours and vicissitudes, are neither insisted upon nor ignored; they are out of the question. The shepherd remains first and foremost an emblem of humanity, a general rather than a specific type, and his afflictions and joys are universal. The process is reversed in the romantic pastoral, which begins with the individual figure, concentrates upon his hard lot in life, and then magnifies him, almost insensibly, into a figure of titanic proportions, an emblem of general Humanity. In modern pastoral, the figure of the shepherd, whether idealized or real, vanishes entirely, his place being taken by some relatively simple figure, sometimes the worker, more usually the child.

If we could say that the earlier pastoral was merely decorative and pretty, however graceful, and the romantic and modern one philosophic and humanitarian, there might be little question as to where our interests and sympathies should lie. But of course the view is not so simple; the Romantics, after all, revolted against the old pastoral in the days of its degeneracy. There is, certainly, a decorative and purely nostalgic tradition in the earlier pastoral, especially in the lyric form, and though its logical conclusion would seem to be in the inanities of Marie Antoinette playing shepherdess at a specially constructed pastoral village at Versailles, it has sometimes won the approbation and sympathy of certain modern critics who see the pastoral as an essentially simple form. The same critics usually deprecate the philosophic, satiric, moral and allegorical pastoral that represents the bulk of complex and serious pastoral art from the ancient world to the later Renaissance. The so-called 'perversion of pastoral' to those profound uses ultimately draws us into the no-man's-land of personal taste, but that does not prevent us from a sifting of the major issues. If the decorative pastoral is really the province of appreciation, the serious pastoral is that of appreciation and what Rossetti called some fundamental brain-work. In a very real sense, all post-Arcadian pastoral is pastoral that has usurped a name; the instincts which give birth to a longing for simplicity are universal in time and place and pastoral may therefore be said to be intrinsic to man's nature, but every private Arcadia created by a modern author or discovered by a modern critic really looks back to the original one as the source of its being. That is why this volume is devoted largely to the complexities of the older pastoral and then (again to limit) to the serious rather than to the decorative pastoral.

There is a third difficulty inherent in defining pastoral. Apart from the question of historical demarcations evident in the lines quoted from Wordsworth, there is another matter evident there, of the forms that pastoral takes, that will bear some scrutiny. In Wordsworth's evocative sketch of pastoral's development, we become aware that it appears not only in the specific form in which it came to birth (the 'Grecian song' or idyll of Theocritus), but that it interpenetrates the drama, as in Shakespeare's *As You Like It* and *The Winter's Tale*; the elegy, as in Spenser's *Astrophel*; and the epic, as in Spenser's *The Faerie Queene*. Expanding upon Wordsworth we could, of course, add to the idyll or eclogue, the pastoral drama and the elegy several other types of pastoral literature: the pastoral lyric extending from the French *pastourelle* of the Middle Ages through the songs of Marlowe and Ralegh and those of Housman and Frost; the pastoral mythological tale or 'minor epic', as in Boccaccio's *Ameto* and Drayton's *Endimion and Phoebe*; the pastoral masque of Sidney, Jonson and Milton; the pastoral novel of Longus, Sannazaro, Sidney and Montemayor; and even (availing ourselves of the broad inclusiveness of the term in our own day) Laurie Lee, the modern British writer whose magical reminiscences of a childhood in Gloucestershire are a prime example of the pastoral of childhood. For each of these cases, therefore, we must find a way to talk about pastoral and its various uses that recognizes that is capable of assuming a form peculiar to itself and also of interpenetrating other forms as a creative element; a way, in other words, that accounts for the capacity of pastoral, traditionally the humblest of poetic forms, to take on various tonalities grander than the shepherd's flute can offer and to marry, frequently and bigamously, above itself.

What emerges from a roll-call of names of writers of pastoral from Theocritus to our own day is an idea of the continuity with variations, the richness and exuberance, of the pastoral conception. In achieving so flourishing an estate, pastoral necessarily suffers from the complication of the terms used to describe it. It has not established itself as the prime term without competition from other terms. In the paragraph immediately above we have spoken variously and indiscriminately of the eclogue, the idyll, the pastoral; and we might have added the bucolic. The idyll is the general descriptive term we use for the poems of Theocritus; derived from the Greek 'eidyllion' (image or picture) it does not define a poetic type so much as to characterize a short poem, descriptive or narrative, which possesses a picturesque or idealistic quality. The eclogue is even less a distinct form of writing: in the original Greek 'eclogē' it means merely a 'selection' from an author's writings, and it may perpetuate the notion of brevity already seen in the idyll. The word bucolic introduces a still vaguer notion: it derives from the Greek 'boukolos', a keeper of cattle as opposed to a shepherd or goatherd, and represents an enhancement of the social status of the figures of pastoral poetry; in our own time it frequently takes on a comic aspect as suggesting a rural lack of sophistication, a comic clumsiness that works to the detriment of the idealistic qualities of both eclogue and idyll.

Pastoral, it then appears, is the most all-embracing of the terms used for this kind of writing, and the fact that it is used in both the singular and the plural leads to a final complication. By pastorals we mean a particular kind of poem: the idylls of Theocritus, the eclogues of Virgil and Spenser, the *Pastorals* of Pope, are all poems of the same formal type, 'mixed' poems of description and dialogue, part-narrative, part-dramatic, and usually but not always in either hexameter or pentameter verse. For critics from the sixteenth to the eighteenth centuries, pastoral in this sense means a particular kind or genre of literature, like Tragedy, Comedy, Satire or Epic, possessing like them its own decorum. More broadly, however, when we speak of pastoral in the singular, we mean really a view of life, an *ethos* or informing principle which can subsist either in itself, as in the poets enumerated above, or which can animate other forms of literature like the drama, whether they be wholly pastoral (as in the case of *As You Like It*) or only partially so (as in the cases of *The Winter's Tale* or *Cymbeline* or *The Tempest*). Hence the word pastoral refers both to form and to content.

The great characteristic of pastoral poetry is that it is written when an ideal or at least more innocent world is felt to be lost, but not so wholly as to destroy the memory of it or to make some imaginative intercourse between present reality and past perfection impossible. As Professor Kermode puts it (*English Pastoral Poetry*, p. 15) pastoral poetry never arises in a time when there are children, as there are now, who have never seen a cow. Pastoral is therefore written from a point of view that we may call sophisticated. Nostalgia cannot be the emotion of those who are not conscious of having experienced a loss, and shepherds therefore do not write pastoral poetry. Were they capable of any kind of poetic production, the probability is that they would write from either a spirit of antagonism to their wretchedness, or a spirit of complacency in their comparative happiness: either alternative would destroy the fragile equilibrium that pastoral maintains. Essentially the art of pastoral is the art of the backward glance, and Arcadia from its creation the product of wistful and melancholy longing. The pastoral poet reverses the process (and the 'progress') of history.

Pastoral's concern with time is what, first and foremost, renders it universal, for it is one of the most deeply rooted instincts of mankind to claim that the world is too much with us and to find an escape from the overwhelming present in a sanctified past or in some indistinct and redeeming future. Those are the only two possible escapes, other than a hedonistic glorification of the present moment itself; the looking forward to the future results in the production of utopian or millennial literature, the looking backward to the past in the Arcadian vision. Pastoral begins with Theocritus remembering his Sicilian boyhood from the perspective of the over-ripe court of Alexandria in the first half of the third century. Pagan in origin, it soon becomes Christian through the happy coincidence of meanings in the word *pastor*, shepherd and priest, and through the influence of pastoral life visible in the Scriptures: the shepherd Abel, the shepherd David, Christ the Good Shepherd, the Lamb of God, the shepherds present at the nativity, the entire pastoral atmosphere of the Song of Songs. The shepherd's life, as Ernst Curtius has noted (p. 187) is a basic form of human existence; it is found in all civilizations and from the beginning. But human life operates constantly in the direction of complexities. In both of our heritages, the classical and the Judaeo-Christian, a pastoral existence is intrinsically bound up with the creation of cities: the shepherd Paris makes a wrong choice and the result is the destruction of one city and, through the dispersal of its inhabitants, the creation of others; Adam in the garden is guilty of another misstep, expulsion follows, and the race of man is sent forth to organize itself into new societies of which the city is the centre. The polar opposite of the open pasture is the confining city, and while it may represent an advance in one way, in another (again the feeling is universal) it is at a terrible cost, and so it perhaps involves a degeneration, no matter how great a testimony it is to man's mastery of arts and sciences unknown to our first father.

The movement from the garden to the city implicit in Christian mythology is a direct result of the Fall, and while every bosom returns an echo to Samuel Johnson's statement that when a man is tired of London he is tired of life, the more orthodox view is stated by Cowper: 'God made the country and man made the town.' The omnipresent desire to escape from the town is really the desire to escape from the circumstances into which we were plunged by the fall and of which the city is, however glorious, really the result. Ultimately, therefore, the dominant idea of pastoral is a search for simplicity away from a complexity represented either by a specific location (Alexandria, Augustan Rome, the courts of Renaissance Italy, Elizabethan or Augustan London) from which the refuge is in a rural retreat to Arcadia; or from a specific period of individual human existence (adulthood), from which the refuge is in the visions of childhood. All pastoral is in search of the original splendour, but the different ways in which it conceives of that splendour are the ground of its fertility and its multiple variations.

In an often-quoted definition that is itself of a complex simplicity, Professor Empson once defined pastoral as essentially the 'process of putting the complex into the simple' (p. 23). In a view with a slightly different emphasis, Professor Kermode sees it as essentially a conflict in terms of Nature and Art (*English Pastoral Poetry*, pp. 37–42). Intrinsically the pastoral is not by the widest stretch of the imagination an escapist literature in the vulgar sense, if only because, as Horace once pointed out and as the eighteenth century was particularly fond of quoting, those who *trans mare currunt*, succeed in changing their skies only, not their inmost souls or their way of thinking. A recourse to Arcadia and the sheephook does not free the inhabitants of the city from their usual perplexities. To arrive in Arcadia by whatever means (and there are many) or for whatever purpose (and the seeking of certain kinds of liberties there may be morally reprehensible) is merely to have one's problems sharpened by seeing them magnified in a new context of simplicity, by seeing Art against Nature and of being forced to conclusions about them. The issues of the great world or of adulthood are transported into Arcadia or into the magic gardens of childhood as to a place and time in which they may be better scrutinized; they are given an objectification by being isolated, and the process may result in a clarification of the motives that bred the desire for escape in the first place. The impulse to pastoral, universal as it is, must inevitably suggest the desire of the weary soul to escape, but the escape, it will become clear, is only temporary and only a prelude to a return. If we have no continuing city, still less do we have a continuing garden.

The contrast between town and country is therefore essential to the rise of a distinctively pastoral art. That same contrast of Art and Nature frequently gives rise to a change from simple lyric celebration of the rural world to satirical, moral or allegorical treatment of the matters imported into the confines of Arcadia and requiring, by their continuing ability to tease the mind even here, an organization and a shape that will render them intelligible. Those who complain of the vitiation of pastoral by the introduction of these foreign or extraneous elements that cloud its pristine loveliness, fail to realize that a note of criticism is inherent in all pastoral from the beginning of its existence. It is latent in the form in its very desire for movement away from an unsatisfactory time and place to another time and place that is imagined to be superior. Satire, moralizing and allegory are merely the inborn tendencies of pastoral rendered overt and explicit. On this question of the importation of foreign matters into the spontaneous lyric beauty of the Arcadian scene, Greg makes a significant remark (p. 67):

The pastoral, whatever its form, always needed and assumed some external circumstance to give point to its actual content. The interest seldom arises directly from the narrative itself. In Theocritus and Sannazaro this objective point is supplied by the delight of escape from the over-civilization of the city; in Petrarch and Mantuan, by their allegorical intention; in Sacchetti and Lorenzo, by the contrast of town and city, with all its delicate humour; in Boccaccio and Poliziano, by the opening it gave for golden dreams of exquisite beauty or

PERSPECTIVES ON THE PASTORAL 13

sensual delight; in Tasso, by the desire of that freedom in love and life which sentimental philosophers have always associated with a return to nature. In all these cases the content *per se* may be said to be a matter of indifference; it only receives meaning in relation to some ulterior intention of the author.

The way in which pastoral adapts itself to various forms is one of our prime concerns. Still, there is a central and unchanging core of meaning in the pastoral convention itself. In all of the examples enumerated by Greg the theme of return is sounded again and again: return to nature, to the primitive simplicity of the Church, to primitive freedom from passion, to primitive enjoyment of passion, to primitive modes of feeling and thinking. The central metaphor to which this theme gives rise is that of the golden age, the consideration of which is the first stage in our survey. Briefly, I propose to treat the subject of pastoral under several main *thematic* headings. Of these, the golden age is the first as representing the general overarching myth of lost innocence which is common to both pagan and Christian traditions of pastoral, to the first by native right, to the second by assimilation to its own myth of the garden of Eden. The perfection of which it is the symbol is imaged in the creation of Arcadia, a paradise for poets which represents the human capacity for idealization even in an iron age or, by analogy, in a postlapsarian state of imperfection. As such, Arcadia represents a midway point between perfection and imperfection, the latter represented by the outer world touching, as Sparta did upon the geographical Arcadia, upon its borders. That world of warfare, ambition, lust and fortune enters and either devastates or annexes the Arcadia of the poet's dreams in the persons of her errant aristocrats. A final brief chapter on the pastoral novel of childhood initiated by Longus's *Daphnis and Chloe* carries us into the modern recreations of the Arcadian dream. This last stage coincides with the pastoral's assumption of another form in the novel; the stage before it with the development of new and elaborate forms of pastoral in the drama, the epic and the pastoral-chivalric romance; and the stage anterior to both with the development of the formal eclogue.

The ancient myth of Arethusa, traditionally the source and patroness of pastoral poetry, is that of a spring which flowed underground from her home in Greece and emerged amid new surroundings in Syracuse; as an emblem of changeful constancy, the myth is especially fitting to the literature it inspires and to the idea central to its being. Constancy with change is precisely the history of pastoral as an informing idea.

2
The Golden Age

The human creature's universal remembrance of a better time finds its chief expression in the myth of the golden age. Hesiod, Virgil, Ovid, Juvenal and Seneca record it fully and in different ways in the classical period; Boethius, Jean de Meung, Dante and Chaucer in the Middle Ages employ it as a metaphor for the age of innocence in Eden; and a host of poets give it renewed life in the Renaissance. Briefly, the chief elements of the myth are these: there is a time at the beginning of human history when Saturn and Astraea, the virgin goddess of justice, dwelt together in the fields of Hesperia, and life for the inhabitants of earth was of the utmost simplicity and beatitude. The earth produced fruits without the cultivation of plough or spade, nectar flowed from the trees spontaneously, and the streams ran with milk. No pine trees were felled to make keels for ships adventuring to foreign lands, no walls surrounded cities, war was unknown. For man, life consisted primarily in leisure and in the free exercise of love which was unconstrained by honour and unclouded by thoughts of shame. Life proceeded in a climate of everlasting spring.

Thus far, as in Milton, with whose description of life in prelapsarian Eden this picture has many connections, man exists in perfect harmony with Nature, his own nature not yet in need of nurture. Two elements predominate: a lack of ambition and aspiration, which implies a virtuous lack of the avarice and pride which are their source; and a desire for sinless pleasure, which in turn implies a virtuous lack of the passion of lust. The golden age establishes both an economic order and a personal freedom which are the twin parts of a single complex of ideas. As we shall see later, one or the other (but particularly the latter) can be isolated and made the subject of a curious emphasis, and Renato Poggioli has referred to them as the 'pastoral of innocence' and the 'pastoral of happiness'.

In Milton, in the ninth book of *Paradise Lost*, this happy state of things is terminated by a Fall which is predicated of two human beings; in the myth of the golden age a degeneration rather than a Fall is asserted; it takes place by degrees only, and it is attributed to the race as a whole, not to single individuals. Saturn is banished, the cycle of the seasons succeeds to the everlasting spring, and the planting of crops begins: we are in the silver age. A further degeneration takes place in the bronze age, which, says Ovid whose *Metamorphoses* is a great *locus classicus* of the idea, is now more prone to have recourse to arms, but is still not wholly impious. But worse is to succeed: the last stage of all is the Iron Age. Men begin to dig for gold, voyages in ships begin for war and trade, common possession of land is renounced in favour of measured boundaries, and conflicts arise within families. The result which symbolizes the entire process is Astraea's desertion of the earth for heaven. Reigning over the entire earth in her place is the spirit of violence and – a phrase that echoes in literature for centuries – *amor sceleratus habendi*, 'the cursed love of gain'.

From the first, therefore, it appears that the lyric celebration of a former time and the nostalgic wistfulness that accompanies it, proceed essentially from a dissatisfaction with, and criticism of, a hideous present. The myth provides an opening for irony and satire. In contrast to Virgil, Ovid and Seneca, Juvenal for example renders its satirical implications overt in his excoriation of the lusts and ambitions of imperial Rome at the beginning of his sixth satire. In the Renaissance, Thomas Howell's lyric 'Of the golden world' plays upon the irony of the goldless golden age with openly satirical effect:

> The golden world is past, saith some,
> But now, say I, that world is come:

> Now all things may for gold be had,
> For gain of gold, both good and bad . . .
> But brief to be, what can you crave
> That now for gold you may not have?
> Then truth to tell, and not to feign,
> Right now the golden world doth reign.

Like pastoral itself, which arises only when an original beauty has been lost, the myth of the golden age arises when gold has only too clearly been discovered.

In the golden age, human life is conceived in terms of the contemplative and the recreative rather than in terms of the active; it is devoted to pleasure and virtuous idleness rather than motivated by ambition. In a word, life in the golden age is pastoral. Shakespeare recalls this aspect of that life when the Duke and his followers in the forest of Arden are said to 'fleet the time carelessly, as they did in the golden world'. Pure *otium*, therefore, has not yet assumed the significance of sloth. Pastoralism and all of its effects are associated with a life anterior to degeneration and pastoral poetry in effect is given a consecration as the poetry of that life. As Michael Drayton put it in his fourth eclogue (1619):

> That simple Age, as simply sung of Love,
> Till thirst of Empire and of Earthly swayes,
> Drew the good Shepheard from his Lasses Glove,
> To sing of slaughter, and tumultuous frayes.

To associate pastoral with the golden age is inevitably to associate heroic poetry, at the other end of the literary scale, with the world of degeneration. If voyages and quests, warfare, soldiering and plundering are the effects of a degeneration, the very literature in which those activities are mirrored, however glamorous with heroism, is itself a testimony of a degeneration. Renaissance authors are always alert to the fact, but no one faced it more squarely or more courageously than Camoens. In his *Lusiads*, the majestic national epic of Portugal, at the very moment when the great expedition of Vasco da Gama, fraught with magnificent destiny, is about to sail (Canto 4), a nameless old man passionately cries out against the entire undertaking, revealing at one and the same time that his creator was aware of a darker side to the heroic gesture and had the artistic integrity to make it part of his total vision:

> O unhappy race, true heirs of that madman whose sin and disobedience not only doomed you to gloomy exile from paradise but drove you from that other divine state of simple, tranquil innocence, the golden age, condemning you in its place to this age of iron and instruments of destruction! Now your fickle fancy has become infatuated with this folly that describes as enterprise and valour what is but the cruel ferocity of the brute creation, and boasts of its contempt for life, which should always be held dear if only because he who gives it was so loath to lose his own.
>
> (tr. William C. Atkinson)

By one view, then, pastoral is the most inferior of the kinds of poetry and especially so in regard of epic, but by another view it can claim a perfection that the other cannot. The need for heroic action stems precisely from the inclination of humankind to evil which began to appear in the ages of silver and bronze, and came to a climax in that of iron. The wrongs that require redress and retribution result at one and the same time in the summoning of armies and the clarion call of heroic poetry that memorializes those musterings. Virgil makes the point about heroic quest and heroic literature in the fourth eclogue. Addressing himself to a mysterious child as yet unborn, with whose birth the golden age will simultaneously return, he tenderly pictures the renewal of the earth but offers no hope of a single and total change in the world; instead, he writes, the metamorphosis will be gradual: another Argo, the ship of the Argonauts in search of the golden fleece, will set out, wars will still be waged, and another Achilles will be sent to Troy once more. And, it is implied, *Argonauticas* and *Iliads* will continue to be written. Lust and avarice, the twin libidinousnesses, will still perturb the world, the rape of Helen and the rape of the golden fleece will still reveal a world no longer golden. Clearly, pastoral and epic imply each other continually.

In the paragraph above, we have already noted the chief difference between the golden age of the pagans and the analogous age in Eden of Christianity. The first is cyclical, it may reappear when the process of history works itself out of the baseness of the iron age. Christianity promises no such general renewal; the Edens that can be recreated are those of the individual soul, the paradise within. Still, the golden age is a convenient and enriching metaphor, and as such it has been used by Christian poets in all times, whenever their subject was the life of Adam in Eden. Both Golding and Sandys, for instance, in their glosses to their translations of the first book of the *Metamorphoses* of Ovid, interpret the golden age in Christian terms, as does Dante before them in the Earthly Paradise set atop the Mountain of Repentance in *Purgatorio*, xxvii:

> Those men of yore who sang the golden time
> And all its happy state – maybe indeed
> They on Parnassus dreamed of this fair clime.
>
> Here was the innocent root of all man's seed,
> Here spring is endless, here all fruits are, here
> The nectar is, which runs in all their rede.
>
> (tr. Dorothy Sayers)

The fusion of the golden age and Eden is made more complex by the introduction of still another element important to pastoral, and it is visible in the fifth and sixth stanzas of Thomas Traherne's lyric 'Eden':

> Only what Adam in his first estate
>   Did I behold;
>   Hard silver and dry gold
> As yet lay underground; my happy fate
>   Was more acquainted with the old
> And innocent delights which he did see
> In his original simplicity.

> Those things which first his Eden did adorn,
>   My infancy
>   Did crown; simplicity
> Was my protection when I first was born.

Here, finally, appear in close conjunction the three dreams of simplicity and felicity which men have universally experienced or imagined: two in space and time, and one in time only. In Traherne, the myth of childhood incorporates the myth of the goldless golden age and that of the stainless beatitude of Eden. All three are overshadowed by a sense of loss and a desire for return.

Time and Nature are the two great abstractions with which serious pastoral art is concerned. The vanishing of the golden Eden not only plunges man into a world of mutability (Shakespeare in *As You Like It* calls it 'the season's difference/The penalty of Adam'), it fundamentally alters his nature. In the orthodox Christian view, human nature, created in a state of perfection, is limited and vitiated by the Fall in the garden. Death enters the world of creation, and the oneness of man with Nature in perfect obedience to the Creator is lost through the irruption of a rooted concupiscence. The hierarchy of reason over passion is inverted by an upsurge from beneath, for which Milton's customary figure is that of usurpation. The consequence is exile from the pastoral garden, exile to a world of toil and labour, and the eternal regretful backward glance of which pastoral is the result. If we return to the garden, therefore, it must be always with an awareness that it was the place of a Fall, and may be so again.

The Fall is therefore the major pre-condition of pastoral poetry, the greatest loss of all. Hence pastoral's double concern for the primitive beginnings of the entire race, and with the primitive beginnings in childhood of the individual. Both man as a type and man as an individual sense that once upon a time they came trailing clouds of glory into the world: the shadows of the prison-house closed in once in Eden, and close in again in every man's progression from the innocent bliss of childhood to adolescence and maturity. In effect, the history of the race is recapitulated in the history of the individual; the youth of mankind finds a parallel in the youth of each man.

Since memory constantly recalls what Henry Vaughan in his poem about Edenic simplicity and childhood 'The Retreate' termed 'Bright *shootes* of everlastingnesse', the question then becomes one of the means by which we can achieve a return to that blissful state. This, in turn, involves two things: in what we consider that first bliss to consist, either innocence or pleasure; and whether it is to be achieved by Nature or Art. In speaking of Nature in this framework of ideas, we mean Nature in two senses: the Nature, innocent and perfect, which was man's before the disaster in the garden, and the Nature to which he was afterwards reduced, limited, corrupted, death-bearing. Prelapsarian nature achieved its goodness and its pleasure naturally, without effort or strain. Postlapsarian nature, on the other hand, is in constant need of correctives – education, law, habit – inculcated rather than springing from within. That is what we mean by Art, a moral skill that is learned. The learning process necessarily involves a certain toil or labour in the intellect which is the counterpart of the physical toil imposed as punishment upon our first parents; like the latter, however, it is also the means to salvation. Perhaps a stanza from Thomas Vaughan's lyric 'The Stone' is the best illustration of the concept:

> Lord God! This a *stone*,
> As *hard* as any One
>   Thy Laws in Nature fram'd:
> 'Tis now a *springing Well*,
> And many Drops can tell,
>   Since it by *Art* was tam'd.

The conflict or co-operation of the two concepts of Nature and

Art is the basis of much of what is to follow. We were speaking of the ways by which humanity perpetually attempts to recapture its first happiness by a re-entry into the garden. If one is in search of a pastoral of happiness only, entry into the garden is facilitated by considering that human nature is still what it was in its original state, that the instinct for fruition is still innocent though wanton. To behave 'naturally' in this sense is in reality to ignore the Fall and its consequences, and to attempt to establish a continuity between his descendants and the unfallen Adam. The libertine instinct creates a paradise out of one aspect only of the original one, and then through a kind of legerdemain of the intellect. The pastoral of innocence works in far different ways. It recognizes Nature for what it is, a fallen state, and calls in the discipline and rule of Art to regulate it in order to achieve the only paradise man can achieve since the Fall, the one within. In this view, there is no question that Nature is superior to the Art so despised by the libertines and primitivists, *if* however we mean by that Nature the one preceding the Fall. Fallen Nature is another matter entirely, and Art is superior to it because it is capable of rectifying it. It is capable of taking a brazen world and rendering a golden one in return. In this sense, Art creates a new Nature; the felicity at which it aims involves transcendence. Instead of looking back wistfully upon the old Paradise it looks to one in the future; as the archangel Michael advises Adam just previous to the expulsion from the garden:

> only add
> Deeds to thy knowledge answerable, add faith,
> Add virtue, patience, temperance, add love,
> By name to come called charity, the soul
> Of all the rest: then wilt thou not be loth
> To leave this Paradise, but shalt possess
> A paradise within thee, happier far.
>
> (*Paradise Lost*, X, 581–7)

The orthodox view accepts a world of fallen innocence together with a necessarily ensuing world of experience in the hope of achieving another innocence on the further side. We have already seen the view expressed in Dante's *Purgatorio*, where the poet's journey leads to the reachievement of the Terrestrial Paradise after the ascent of the Mountain of Repentance. The achievement is made through spiritual labour and an education supervised, in this particular case, by both Reason and Revelation in the persons of Virgil and Beatrice. A similar idea occurs in Book IV of Castiglione's *The Courtier*, in the discussion centring about the cardinal virtues in general and temperance in particular. The application of these to the ruler's mind will give him, it is said there, 'the manner and method of right rule: which of itself alone would suffice to make men happy and to bring back once again to earth that Golden Age which is recorded to have existed once upon a time when Saturn ruled' (tr. C. Singleton).

In so far as it begins with a longing for a world of rural simplicity from the perspective of an over-sophisticated environment, all pastoral poetry, initially at least, expresses a preference for Nature over Art. This is what we might call the pre-condition of pastoral. By Renaissance poets the court is seen as the heart of the city and as a microcosm of its evils; a move to rural retirement represents a search for the recovery of innocence. The multitudes of complaints against court life to which the great centres of Europe gave rise all lead in this direction. They represent a mingling of Juvenalian attacks upon civil corruption with an Horatian admiration for the restricted ambitions and moderated appetites of country existence. Wyatt's two poems, 'Of the mean and sure estate' and 'Of the courtier's life' are poems of this kind, praising the *aurea mediocritas* of the country and indicating why the poet prefers to the slippery existence of the courtier the pleasures of being 'in Kent and Christendom, /Among the Muses'. There is, furthermore, a whole set of courtly lyrics that have none of the usual trappings of pastoral but are essentially akin to it in their praise of inner quiet. They range from Edward Dyer's 'My mind to me a kingdom is' to Thomas Dekker's 'Art thou poor, yet hast thou golden slumbers?' to Robert Greene's 'Sweet are the thoughts that savor of content'. And there are, finally, the famous monologues in Shakespeare's *Henry VI*, Part III (II, v, 1–54) and *Henry V* (IV, i, 234–88) in which royal perturbations are contrasted with rural serenity, a feeling that if developed in another direction results as a matter of course in pastoral art.

In looking to the rural world for an escape from civilization, these poets isolate the aspect of the golden age that the erotic poets wholly ignore, its freedom from tumult and strife. To return to Nature for them signifies a return to simple and innocent behaviour and manners. Ultimately, of course, it is a simple view, and it is not a complete view, but it represents at least a movement in the right direction, for the perspective gained on court life from the country may lead in the end to its restoration.

The important thing to notice about these poets who stress the calm of the retired life is that they say nothing about the country as an arena for love and for the free exercise of the sexual instinct. For them, the return to Nature is not motivated by erotic desire and the liberation of feeling but by social complications too great to be borne. In contrast, in the poets of the erotic tradition the attitude of being at one with Nature usually brings in the idea of being as morally innocent, as luxuriant and generous as Nature herself. The view is that commonly put into the mouths of the great seducers in Renaissance love poetry, from Marlowe's Leander through Shakespeare's Venus to Milton's Comus, and it is always undermined by a current of irony. Those who conceive of Art as inferior to Nature usually conceive of man as still living in a pre-lapsarian state, and therefore of being able to recapture its blisses at will. It is not surprising to find a sentimental view of human nature as innocent and sinless in its desire for pleasure flowering in its most elaborate form in the poetry of love. If one way of regaining the lost paradise is by repentance, virtuous conduct and simplicity of life, the other way is by an unbridled enjoyment of 'natural' instincts. In its provision of leisure for such an enjoyment, the pastoral life is the most suitable sphere for such a conception. It was after all the great *magister amoris* Ovid himself who warned that if you take *otia* away, Cupid's bows will be broken.

The pastoral of happiness gives rise to two different viewpoints, one in which Nature is upheld as the universal law, and one in which Art is similarly advanced. One of the places where the confrontation between the two views is most clearly visible has long been noted in the history of pastoral. Indeed, it is impossible to miss it owing to the almost absolute similarity of the two forms in which it occurs, the two choruses on the golden age in the two greatest pastoral dramas of the Italian High Renaissance, Tasso's *Aminta* and Guarini's *Il Pastor Fido*. The similarity exists because Guarini challenged Tasso's entire conception of that golden time and utilized his predecessor's own images and terms, his very metre and rhymes, to assert an entirely different intellectual position.

The two choruses are lyric statements on the subject of love in the golden age, and they are remarkable not only for their great beauty but also for their isolation of the love-element which we noted as only one aspect of the desirability of that primeval time of bliss. For Tasso, who asserts in terms of high rapture a purely naturalistic view of life and love in that happy time, the golden age is golden not because of the spontaneous abundance of the earth nor for its freedom from war, but *solely* because that 'idol of errors, idol of deceit' that is called Honour by the 'insane mob' had not yet made its appearance amid the 'amorous flock' of lovers. The law of Nature known to those happy souls was, he sings, the golden and felicitous one she had sculpted into their hearts: '*S'ei piace, ei lice*', licit if pleasing. The final three-line conclusion to the

five strophes of which the poem is composed summarizes this theme
by the invocation of a Catullan reminiscence that fuses a *carpe
diem* sentiment with a note of exquisite melancholy:

> Amiam: che'l Sol si muore e poi rinasce;
> A noi sua breve luce
> S'asconde, e'l sonno eterna notte adduce.
>
> [Love while we may; the sun will sink and rise;
> But our brief light once gone,
> He hides, and sleep draws endless midnight on.]

The resolution therefore, though more plangent, is like that of
Marvell's in 'To his Coy Mistress': if we cannot stay the course of
the sun, let us speed up its motion in a rapid round of pleasures
that blur the effect of time; the present moment swallows the past
and the future and in effect becomes both.

Guarini's response to this is to render the golden age in strictly
moralistic terms, as a time which is golden precisely for the reasons
that Tasso denies *and also* for the fact that a 'lawful flame' was
kindled in nymphs and swains. Thus love is subordinated and
moralized, not isolated and liberated as in Tasso. The point of the
most direct challenge is obscured in Sir Richard Fanshawe's magnificent translation of 1647, and therefore I rely upon my own for
Guarini as previously for Tasso. Where Tasso had written of the
law of Nature as '*S'ei piace, ei lice*', Guarini has the inexorable and
succinct '*Piaccia, se lice*', pleasing if lawful. In the one case Nature is
exalted over Art (lawfulness, licitness), in the other that hierarchy
is reversed and the elements are no longer at strife but co-operating
in harmony. Less original, less great as poetry, Guarini's rendering
of the theme is nevertheless the more orthodox and traditional. His
conclusion, moreover, invokes, not a pagan precedent in Catullus,
but the Christian tradition of life after death:

> Speriam, che il sol cadente anco rinasce,
> E'l Ciel, quando men luce,
> L'aspettato seren spesso n'adduce.

[Let's live in hope; declining suns arise;
Heaven's light is almost gone
At dawn, which leads desired daylight on.]

We may notice in passing that in 'Lycidas' Milton also invokes this traditional motif of the sun from pagan erotic poetry and elevates it into a symbol of Resurrection.

The tendency to escape, under the stress of a desire for a life of 'pure' instinct, not only from the effects but also from the very idea of a Fall, is very strongly expressed in the chorus of Tasso. It would be a pleasure to assume that our instincts were always happy, hearty and wholesome, that between the desire and its fruition no consideration of its licitness need intervene. However, that there may be the possibility at least of an intentional irony in Tasso's verses is not to be lightly dismissed. The court that heard these sentiments expressed at its first performance was a court enjoying itself in its lighter moments, but it was nevertheless a Christian court of post-Tridentine Italy. Moreover, there is a subtle indication at the most crucial point of the natural not being wholly natural but a mixture of art and nature: Nature *sculpts* her law into the heart of the swains of the golden age. The vision of the unfallen world must be expressed, *can* be expressed, only in the language of a fallen world that saw the creation of the arts.

In that case, Guarini's chorus is only a rendering overt of what is implicit in Tasso's, a recall to deliberation from a momentary enthusiasm that knows itself to be enthusiasm in its graver moments. The same situation occurs in the relationship between what is most probably the single most famous pastoral lyric in English and the two poems written in response to it, Marlowe's joyous 'The Passionate Shepherd to his Love', Ralegh's gravely moral 'The Nymph's Reply to the Shepherd', and Donne's openly satirical 'The Bait'.

With the exception that the speaker is himself a shepherd and not a knight, the Marlowe lyric is analogous in its situation to the

c

medieval *pastourelle*, a lyric form recounting the chance encounter of a chivalric adventurer and a shepherdess and the invitation by the former to a moment of delight that is most often refused. The *pastourelle* reveals that mixture of two classes of society in a pastoral setting that will concern us later when pastoral becomes chivalric in the great prose romances of the sixteenth century. 'The Passionate Shepherd to his Love' presents a very ambiguous situation, for while the figure who proffers the invitation presumably inhabits the world of natural simplicity, the artfulness of his address and the sophistication of his gifts (not cheeses or flowers or pipes) mark him as not altogether a simple figure. His birds sing, not native wood-notes wild, but the very complicated part-songs called madrigals. He offers 'buckles of the purest gold', 'coral clasps and amber studs', articles not commonly within reach of his class. And his limitation of experience to spring mornings is a lovely oblivion of the natural cycles of time. The mixture of the worlds of Nature and Art is suspicious and the invitation to a world of unadulterated delight and idleness confirms that suspicion. The lyric loveliness of the poem therefore seems to contain its own irony, a complexity suspended in apparent simplicity. The shepherdess in Marlowe is not allowed a reply. That is what Ralegh undertakes to give, by rendering explicit the implications of the shepherd's invitation in a Guarini-like rehandling of Marlowe's setting, imagery and rhymes. For whenever in the Renaissance someone undertakes to sing in the Horatian or Catullan strain of *carpe diem*, he is sure to hear a whisper at his ear of '*Eheu, fugaces*'. Both moods spring from the same consciousness of time's passing, but the hedonist makes an eternity of the moment that turns past, present and future into one, while the moralist is careful to distinguish between them. When love seeks to recreate the golden age as it once existed and never will exist again, the only appeal is to the facts of time and mutability that spring from the loss in the garden. To the 'May morning' of Marlowe Ralegh opposes the figure of Time driving the flocks from summer field to winter fold; to the madrigals of the melodious birds, the songs of Philomel, memorializing an ancient wrong of changed affections, rape and murder. The poem is altogether more sombre, terse and gnomic in its effects than we could have expected, but its very gravity is an indication of the large issues underlying the slight lyric grace of the poem to which it is a response. Ralegh's poem holds the same regret from which Marlowe's poem springs ('could youth last', 'Had joys no date') but it sees the world as decidedly fallen; the way to felicity is not the way backward in time.

The third poem in the sequence goes even further to assert the fact of a Fall and thereby to render explicit the implicit hedonism in Marlowe. It does so by an ironic and humorous bit of self-mockery: these lovers are not content with ordinary kinds of bliss, they seek the creation of 'new pleasures'. Taking off from the situation as it is initially found in Marlowe, Donne cunningly transfers the setting from a pastoral to a piscatorial setting. This startling occurrence requires a brief glance at a peculiar development in pastoral in the earlier sixteenth century. Pastoral is concerned almost exclusively with the life of shepherds, but one of the idylls of Theocritus (XXI) glances at the life of fisher-folk, at least as simple and ruminative as shepherds, if not so given to songfulness or amatory pursuits. However, the wholesale shift of the setting from its usual fields and meadows to the seaside occurs in the Neapolitan poet Sannazaro in his Latin *Piscatory Eclogues*; the poems set a fashion for two centuries, of which the most successful example was the seashore idylls of Phineas Fletcher in the earlier seventeenth century.

Donne demonstrates his awareness of this pastoral-piscatorial tradition, but his transfer to a seaside setting is made with cunning and malice, and for reasons of his own. Though the speaker is again the male, the woman is fully in control of the situation by the open submission of her lover, and the result is that he is likened to fish who betray themselves into the net. There is probably an ironic glance here at the Biblical 'fishers of men', and certainly an allusion to the usual representation of the *Meretrix* of Renaissance emblem-books as a woman, horned like a goat, drawing in a netful of fish; Shakespeare's Cleopatra is also portrayed as a cunning fisher of men (II, v, 8 ff.) and Tasso's enchantress Armida quite literally converts her cast-off lovers into fish (X, 66). The changes in setting, characterization and tone force us to measure the distance we have travelled from an apparently simple pastoral situation to a much more explicitly ironic development. The three lyrics hold, as in a state of distillation, a good many of the major issues to which the concept of love in the golden age gives rise.

So far we have been concerned with an essentially lyric expression of these ideas, for they lend themselves particularly to that form. When they pass into narrative, they are capable of illuminating areas of human experience, particularly if the experience is that of romantic love. Marlowe's *Hero and Leander* is not a pastoral poem by any of the usual standards, though it is a tale of primitive instincts aiming at fruition but smoothed over by a careful art to appear like primal and untutored innocence. The great wittiness of the poem arises from just such a clash of naturalness and artfulness, and the long speech beginning at line 199 of the First Sestiad in which Leander uses the most consummate art to persuade Hero of the essential innocence and naturalness of his desires, is a focus of that clash. His arguments are the common ones of the libertine naturalist striving to recreate the golden age of freedom in love, and it is not surprising to find that the golden age is directly referred to at the end of the first part of the poem. Just after the lovers have made arrangements for their first meeting by night, the main narrative breaks off, and Marlowe introduces, in Ovidian fashion, a tale within a tale that takes up over a hundred lines and has customarily been treated as an amusing but inessential excrescence. The tale concerns the love of Mercury for a shepherdess and is therefore both mythological and pastoral in focus. It is told ostensibly to explain why the Destinies, to whom Cupid in the main narrative flies to beg success for the hero and heroine's love, are inimical to him and to love. The narrative is involved and requires a brief summary: Mercury once fell in love with a country maid who spurned him – 'lofty pride that dwells/In towered courts is oft in shepherds' cells' – but ultimately succumbed to his entreaties and set him a task to prove his love, which was to steal nectar from Jove to make her immortal ('All women are ambitious naturally'). Mercury complies with the request, Jove thrusts him out of heaven, and he complains to Cupid who causes the Destinies to dote on Mercury and dethrone his oppressor. The narrative then moves to its climax:

> They granted what he craved, and once again
> Saturn and Ops began their golden reign.

Love has succeeded, it would appear, in recreating the golden age, romantic love can flourish freely once again, and 'Murder, rape, war, lust and treachery' vanish with Jove into the 'Stygian empery'. But the final irony follows immediately upon this peculiar restoration of the golden time by such suspicious means as Cupid uses. The second golden age is incredibly brief ('But long this blessed time continued not'), for Mercury, as if in proof of Ralegh's strictures about the failure of youth to last, love to breed, or truth to be in shepherd's tongues, turns reckless of his promise to the Destinies, despises their love, and the result is the second downfall of Saturn and the re-exaltation of Jupiter with all the evils of his reign.

The obvious point about the narrative is, of course, that the Destinies are now inimical to Cupid and, since he fosters the love of Hero and Leander, that love is bound to be tragic in its end. But the involved tale is not merely an inflated piece of pastoral-mythological decoration. It is related thematically to the main narrative. The love of Hero and Leander pretends to recreate the golden age by feigning that it operates in an atmosphere of untainted purity. 'My words', says Leander, 'shall be as spotless as my youth/Full of simplicity and naked truth', and he immediately proceeds to one of the most expert rhetorical assaults upon virginity before *Comus*. His love proffers itself as purely 'natural' but his arguments that virginity is to be used constantly employ examples from the world of art: ships are useless unless they sail, vessels of brass are made to be handled, treasure is sterile unless it is 'put to loan'. The primitive instinct for possession and fruition, trying to assert itself as untainted and natural, inevitably expresses itself in terms of artfulness, undoing itself in the process with magnificent comic irony. As a 'nun' of Venus's church, Hero is well equipped to appraise a love that aims purely (the pun is intended) at consummation. It carries the seeds of its own destruction within it from the first.

The employment of Art to pretend that Nature is innocent and that therefore there is no need of Art to control it carries its own failure with it, its own comedy, its own irony: human illusions constantly give rise to all of them. Basically, it involves the use of reason to corrupt reason. The theme occurs, with many of the themes treated in the present section, in an epic poem which again is not essentially pastoral, but which constantly incorporates themes to which pastoral gives rise, particularly those of the golden age and of Nature and Art. The second book of *The Faerie Queene*, the Legend of Temperance, deals with the golden age in two of its greatest passages, in the encounter of Guyon with Mammon in canto VII and again in the encounter with Acrasia in the Bower of Bliss in canto XII. Both tempt with gold, the former by appealing to avarice, the other by appealing to lust in an earthly paradise where even the leaves on the trees are gold. In Mammon's cave, the gold is real, palpable, the precious metal itself stamped into coins and ingots; in Acrasia's bower, it is fashioned to represent natural objects like ivy or grapes. Acrasia's represents the more subtle attack upon the hero, for her garden, which is a garden of love in which the refrain of 'gather ye roses' constantly resounds, utilizes gold as a symbol for the liberation of passion: in a literal interpretation of the golden qualities of the golden age, it employs gold to suggest that nature is yet unfallen and that men still can live in a golden time when the impulse to passion is in need of no restraint. The Bower of Bliss is based largely on the descriptions of the gardens of the enchantress Armida in Tasso's *Jerusalem Delivered*, and it is interesting to note that Tasso openly equates the garden with the golden age. One of its lovely inhabitants greets the soldiers who have come to recall Rinaldo from his life of dereliction amid its enchantments with the words: 'O happy men! that have the grace . . ./This bliss, this heav'n, this paradise to see', and then continues significantly:

> This is the place wherein you may assuage
> Your sorrows past, here is that joy and bliss
> That flourished in the antique golden age.

(XV, 62–3; tr. Edward Fairfax)

Like Tasso's, Spenser's gardens are a parody of the golden age, not the age itself. Its climate is one of perpetual spring; a place of intemperance, its air is ironically free of scorching heat or 'cold intemperate'. The heavens themselves over this place of immoderate pleasure look down upon the pleasant bowers 'with season moderate/Gently attempred' to its inhabitants.

The entire place is one in which Art is employed viciously rather than creatively, to suggest an original innocence that has for ever departed, and which Art itself, in its better uses, should strive to recreate in a wholly different way. Art usurps Nature here in an attempt to look like Nature herself and to conceal the fact that this is not another Eden but a garden of corruption at whose centre sits a Venus-like figure of dissoluteness drawing the life slowly but inexorably from an idle and derelict soldier. Guyon destroys the gardens because he sees them for what they are, a wilful and parodic attempt to elude reality. His uncharacteristic and sudden outburst of violence is the result of self-knowledge; he is by now the embodiment of Temperance, a virtue that involves the right rule of oneself and which can restore the golden age in the only way in which it can truly be restored, a way diametrically opposite to that of wistful and sentimental hedonism.

Guyon can recognize the falsity of the golden age recreated through Acrasia's pastoral of happiness because he has previously been called upon to assert the reality of the pastoral of innocence. In his descent into Mammon's cave, his refusal to be tempted by riches and treasures occasions an angry outburst from his tempter. Why, Mammon inquires, in response to Guyon's long rehearsal of the woes to which the desire for riches gives birth, does humankind then weary itself constantly in an acquisitive quest for gain? Guyon's answer that intemperance is the cause leads him to a reflection upon the origins of those double perturbations of lust and avarice (symbolized of course by Acrasia and Mammon) in the fall from a golden age to an iron age:

> The antique world, in his first flowring youth,
> Found no defect in his Creators grace,
> But with glad thankes, and unreproved truth,
> The guifts of soveraine bounty did embrace:
> Like angels life was then mens happy cace:
> But later ages pride, like corn-fed steed,
> Abusd her plenty and fat swolne encreace
> To all licentious lust, and gan exceed
> The measure of her meane, and naturall first need.
>
> Then gan a cursed hand the quiet wombe
> Of his great grandmother with steele to wound,
> And the hid treasures in her sacred tombe
> With sacriledge to dig. Therein he fownd
> Fountaines of gold and silver to abownd,

Of which the matter of his huge desire
And pompous pride eftsoones he did compownd;
Then avarice gan through his veines inspire
His greedy flames, and kindled life-devouring fire.

(VII, 16–17)

It is inevitable that to a mind like Mammon's, the golden age will take on the aspect of a rude time of deprivation that no man of sense and sophistication will seek to restore. He too, like Acrasia, to whom he is closely linked, strives to recreate a golden age in literal terms. For him, the degeneration from the golden age is reality, but it is one in which he rejoices as representing an advance over a 'state forlorne'. Chiefly in that does he differ from Guyon, who, accepting the Fall as a reality and knowing that the golden age can never be renewed in its original form, nevertheless recognizes that it may be re-established by the virtue of which he is in process of becoming the embodiment. The backward glance of longing at the golden age is an absolute essential to provide a sense of direction in our search for our recovery of it; as time advances, it recedes ever further and further, and yet it beckons from ahead.

In defining the condition of postlapsarian man, Guyon accepts his own limitations as a human being, recognizing both the results of the Fall in the freeing of the passions of lust and avarice and also the need for Art to establish an active control over them. Gradually he learns the necessity for moral skill, and it is notable that when he enters the Bower of Bliss, we see him 'Brydling his will and maystering his might', a figure by which Spenser reminds us that the commonest representation of Temperance in the Middle Ages and Renaissance was a woman holding a bridle.

The sense of toil and struggle necessary to virtuous conduct visible here in the figure of bridling has been prefigured by several other passages in Book II in which themes common to pastoral occur. In Bragadocchio's conversation with Belphoebe (III, 39–42) and again in Phaedria's incantatory lulling of Cymochles

(VI, 15–17) there is expressed the old conflict between rural retirement and service at court, pleasure and indolence and labour and involvement. These are themes that in a fuller treatment will occupy us later in Sidney and in Spenser, but here it may suffice to note an important point that will later be developed. Pastoral retirement is, of and in itself, not necessarily good or evil; it depends on the personage involved. For Bragadocchio, being in the country and being at court produce no fundamental change of personality; for him the court is a place where one may swim in pleasure, the country a place which offers a convenient opportunity for a solitary rape. The retirement from which Bragadocchio scornfully invites Belphoebe before attempting to assault her is, on the other hand, a sphere entirely proper to her. As Spenser will say in Book VI, 'It is the mynd that maketh good or ill.' As we shall see later, those representatives of the chivalric world who wander into the Arcadian sunlight come in search of retirement and refreshment, but the length of their stay is marked, and it is really a place where a choice of life is offered to them: contemplative *otium* preparatory to active engagement in the world or a derelict sloth in flight from the world's great issues. The corruption-ridden courts which have initiated their flight summon them back to make their contemplative vision a practical thing in the restoration of a fallen society; they summon them as Gloriana's quest summons Redcrosse Knight from an inappropriate desire to move wholly into the world of contemplation and to remain there in forgetfulness of his destiny. We have anticipated ourselves, however, in our mention of the Arcadian world, and we must first sketch the scenery of that mental country before it finally begins to fill with those alien figures.

3
Arcadia
and its Transformations

The land of Arcadia is really the landscape of an idea. The golden haze diffused through its summer air is ultimately a long reflection of the intenser light of the golden age. When it most preserves those splendours, Arcadia functions as an idyllic world of leisure, poetry and felicitous love which mankind can conceive of even in an impoverished fallen state, and which represents the human potential in its highest reaches. The only combats it knows are those of the shepherd *conflictus* in hours of idleness, a poetic rivalry whose theme is the superiority of one shepherdess to another, and which is motivated by a hope of gain aiming at nothing more precious than a beechen bowl, a lamb, a pipe. When, as happens frequently, Arcadia darkens with recollections of an external world of hard reality, that leisure becomes monotony, the poetry turns into complaint and elegy, and love, thwarted of fulfilment, becomes desire for death. Only simplistically is Arcadia viewed as a perfectly blissful place, for even there, as Panofsky has shown, death intrudes and the note of disaster in Nature is sounded. Paradoxically, however, disaster in love and disaster in death lead to the new creation of poetry. Arcadia is primarily the paradise of poetry. It is a middle country of the imagination, half-way between a past perfection and a present imperfection, a place of Becoming rather than Being, where an individual's potencies for the arts of life and love and poetry are explored and tested. It points two ways therefore, backward into the past and forward into a possible future.

The assumption of the pastoral stance represents a coming to terms with complexity by retiring temporarily to a position of comparative simplicity. That another complexity and another simplicity results is in the nature of things. We know that human beings cannot bear very much reality, and the consequence, especially in the arts in which it undertakes to examine the complexities of that existence, is a continuous series of conventions that paradoxically make them both more distant and more proximate. Arcadia represents just such a convention, a convention rooted in paradox, in which an order is imposed on the flux of reality by removing it to another setting entirely that it may be shaped and governed. The assumption of the shepherd's weeds and the entrance into Arcadias of the mind reveal that a poet can conceive of two ways at least of looking at himself and at reality, at complex matters from the perspective of simplicity, at simplicity itself from the point of view of the complex. The sympathy for other ways of life and thought, the capacity for self-appraisal, the lack of rigidity in the personality implied by such a gesture all augur well for the future development of that personality. Part-playing is a necessary part of all life, though a mind of puritanical cast will frequently see it as evidence of a lack of integrity: witness the modern emphasis on simple 'sincerity'. But if we are so unshakeably rooted to a conception of ourselves and that conception is assaulted and overthrown, the destruction of the personality may be the inevitable result. But to be able to imagine several positions rather than one is the hallmark of a larger and more buoyant mind and of a more engaging personality as well. We cannot imagine, for example, the stiff inelasticity of Malvolio in the pastoral setting to which Rosalind so easily accommodates herself.

Our attitudes towards the kind of convention Arcadia represents are themselves frequently only a convention. On the face of it, the physical manifestation of Arcadia is a lovely absurdity of deodorized Damons and suspiciously fragrant Phyllises, and it customarily evokes from our own modern convention of realism, which thinks it renders the thing itself with no illusionary veils, only a patronizing and derisive laughter. In its central idea, however, Arcadia in its manipulation and re-manipulation through the centuries, voices a universal human situation. Since humanity changes, conventions (Arcadia among them) also change: Samuel Johnson's notorious judgement on the Arcadian atmosphere of 'Lycidas' was that it was easy, vulgar and disgusting. But consider, in the world of reality itself, what conventions for the proper exhibition of grief are thought suitable in modern London, say, or rural Ireland, or central Sicily. Our lives are bounded by conventions at every point, and our literature reflects them constantly. The concern of this chapter, then, is the birth, modification, death and reappearance of Arcadia over a span of nearly two thousand years, and its central focus is the Renaissance rendition of that interior landscape.

In a superb chapter on Virgil, Bruno Snell has taught us to see Arcadia as a spiritual landscape discovered by the Roman poet, himself not the creator of pastoral poetry but a successor to the Syracusan Theocritus in whose work it first appears. The world with which Theocritus is concerned is the idyllic one of a lush and summer-ripe Sicily, remembered from his boyhood and viewed in idealizing memory from the perspective of the overblown civilization of the Alexandria of Ptolemy Philadelphus. The thirty idylls collected under his name are neither all by him, nor all pastorals. Some are panegyrics, love-poems, epithalamia, or brief scenes from epics treated in the decorative manner prescribed by Callimachus. Of the pastorals proper, only one, the seventh, 'The Harvest Festival', appears to introduce actual acquaintances of the poet in a pastoral guise. Over all the pastorals, there is a glow of good humour which sometimes reaches into a delicate irony: it is the townsman's dream of the country, content with the dream and no more. No one ever recorded that pastoral nostalgia propelled Theocritus into action to leave Alexandria and recover the simple delights of his boyhood. Pastoral never does; its very nature is to arouse ambivalent feelings. Speaking of Theocritus taking pains to present a realistic picture of rural life while at the same time preserving a literary mood, Snell writes (p. 286): 'All this is done in a spirit of good-natured jesting; the dissonance between the bucolic simplicity of the pasture and the literary refinement of the city is never completely resolved, nor was it ever intended to be, for the whole point of Theocritus's humour lies in this dissonance.' The dissonance is a way of preserving a dream in the face of the rigours of logic and actuality, an escape-hatch which keeps fantasy alive. The sense of ambivalence in Theocritus derives mainly from his use of an ordered and sophisticated language to voice the doings and sayings of the Sicilian shepherds, for while the language of his hexameters is the rustic and antiquated Doric, that Doric itself is largely an artificial creation of the poet's, eclectic and invented (Gow, p. xxiii). In a word, the antithesis of Art and Nature is visible in terms of language, not of theme, and it is from that fact that the irony arises from Theocritus's contemplation of simplicity. That irony, gentled by sentiment, grows to its greatest proportions in Idyll XI, in which the grotesquely ugly Cyclops, Polyphemus, addresses a tender love-complaint to a nymph who has spurned him. By removal to the pastoral world, even the ugly and the grotesque achieve a kind of charm.

In Theocritus we find the sources of much that is transfigured in Virgil: the emphasis on love and death, singing and song-contest in the pastorals proper, along with a single notable instance of allegory; and in the poems which are not pastorals at all, a pane-gyric and epic mood which will become part of the pastoral fabric in Virgil. The originality of the Roman consists precisely in this fusing and harmonizing of themes in a pastoral setting which absorbs and as-similates them. An original complexity has been further augmented.

To Virgil, as Snell so brilliantly demonstrates, Sicily was too real a place to be romantic; it had fallen within the orbit of Roman greatness and since the charm to Roman ears of names like Daphnis and Tityrus lay precisely in their being foreign and exotic, the habitation chosen for them by a Roman could only be a distant one. Theocritus's removal in distance and time from his Sicilian boyhood is augmented by Virgil's cultural removal from his predecessor's life and landscape. We are at two removes instead of one, and the sense of distance which is the essential of pastoral is immeasurably heightened. In receding from their source, Virgil's pastoral poems are already in process of creating a literary tradition of artifice. The result is the choice of a location already reputed to be characterized by its inhabitants' predilection for poetic contests, that portion of Greece that borders on Sparta, Arcadia. The Arcadia known to geographers is wholly unprepossessing, an area delimited by mountains and crossed by ridges, but its olden designation as the home of Pan and its reputation for a simple rural poetry rendered it suitable for a pastoral art at two removes from reality. The poetry of the Arcadians was not, of course, pastoral; it lacks the sense of distance from the simple world that is pastoral's chief characteristic. In choosing Arcadia, Virgil chooses an imaginary world which represents the projection of an ideal: the Arcadia of his eclogues represents a conflation of Sicilian with Northern and Southern Italian landscapes, a union of reality and idealism which works to the idealization of all three. It becomes a universal.

Evoked from a greater distance in time and space, the Arcadian landscape is necessarily for Virgil a place of lyricism and tender sentiment, a creation of his own. He ignores or misses the gentle irony of Theocritus's over-educated shepherds and accepts them at face value as evidence of a lovelier past. Into his recreation of their lives he instils a deeper emotional and spiritual note from which the delicate humour of Theocritus, closer to his subject and therefore more appraising, is almost wholly missing. To be sure, there exist in the *Eclogues* all kinds of situations that could lend themselves to irony: the Tityrus to whom Meliboeus complains about the loss of his farm is almost callously unconcerned with anything but his own joy at having preserved his own; the adored Alexis whose favours Corydon has lost to the richer Iollas is a haughty little catamite who sells to the highest bidder; the song-match between Menalcas and Damoetas is born from an ill-tempered quarrel that disrupts the peace of the pastoral world. Still, these are situations resolved by the pastoral atmosphere itself, in which some at least find joy: the loss of one farm or love can be balanced by the gain of another and the harmony of a song grows out of a discord. It is not a perfect world, not a golden age, but it is better than the world we all know is without. Virgil has a paradoxical sense of being in proximate detachment from his subject; a mood of interiority arises from an endeavour to reach out and possess and acclimatize the strange and unfamiliar. It is the mood of one trying to remember what was never really known. The *Eclogues* are not merely a subconscious reverie over the long-ago and far-away. The process of art is fully conscious, and this fact we may recognize in the deliberate alterations Virgil makes in what he obviously already conceives of as a literary tradition. He complicates the contrast of simplicity and sophistication by adopting an even more noticeably inappropriate diction for his shepherds: far more than those of Theocritus, his Arcadians live, in Snell's apt phrase, beyond their intellectual means.

Because Virgil's Arcadia is an abstraction as Theocritus's Sicily was not, it allows a great intermingling of figures from the different worlds of reality and idea. Gods, shepherds and men from the world of outer reality all meet and mingle in the pastoral world (the tenth eclogue is the consummate example) and a great step forward into allegory has been taken. The meeting of gods, shepherds and men brings together the three worlds which are present either obviously or by implication in the *Eclogues*: the world of Arcadia itself, the golden world which has departed for ever, and the Roman world of actuality beyond the borders, a world from which poets (and it appears poets only) gain access to Arcadia. Arcadia

itself is the encompassing image of the other two. From the perspective of Arcadia the poet can visualize the golden age in all its
past glory (Eclogue IV) and postulate its cyclical return (through
the birth of a mysterious child that later ages identified with the
Saviour) in the near future. The note of eschatology that Virgil
introduces here broadens the scope of Arcadia from this time on.
Another broadening aspect appears from the other direction, for the
intrusion of the world of ambition and politics, war and injustice
that is contemporary Rome appears at the very beginning of the
collection, in the first eclogue, where Virgil memorializes the dis-
possession from their farms of the supporters of Antony who had
lost to Octavian. The way from historical and personal or political
allegory is not long. In all cases, then, Virgil's discovery of Arcadia is the discovery of a realer and more intense reality than life
can offer, and its very timelessness and placelessness accommodate
all time, past, present and future, and all place. Arcadia is itself
mental time, mental place.

The subjects of love, death and poetry are the most constant
and characteristic elements of Arcadia, and they appear as the love-
complaint, the elegy and the poetic contest of alternating song
which goes by the name amoebean. Of the three, poetry is surely
the most important, for in effect it creates from the other two, and
is conscious at all times of doing so. In Virgil, the wholly new view
of Arcadia as a place of retirement for poets and members of their
circle leads naturally to a new view of poetry as a self-conscious art,
aware of itself as a process rather than a product. The question to
which deliberate pastoral retirement gives rise for a poet is, to
what end poetry? Theocritus, as we saw, is content to narrate
epic events or situations in as brief a compass as his pastorals:
hence the name idyll for both. The political atmosphere of his
age, recovering from the epic conquests of Alexander, together
with the literary tradition established by himself and Callimachus,
made epic endeavour and epic poetry on a large scale seem both

out of date and impracticable. There is no drive towards a higher strain of song in Theocritus. Virgil, however, initiates a kind of programme for poetry, and his example serves as a spur to a number of poets who at one time or another either contemplated or achieved the epic and were all originally Arcadians, Sannazaro, Spenser, Milton and Pope.

On three occasions in the *Eclogues*, at the beginning of the fourth, sixth, and eighth, we are made aware that Virgil can at least conceive of, though he does not immediately move to, a world of epic endeavour apart from a life of retirement, and of a poetic celebration of that world in another more appropriate style than that of pastoral. The different life is the active one as opposed to the contemplative, the different poetry is the heroic as opposed to the pastoral. The eschatology of the fourth eclogue induces him to a change of tone ('*paulo maiora canamus*'), the Epicurean cosmology of the sixth is introduced by an apology: 'Now, Varus, since bards enough will volunteer to sing your praises and to compose the unhappy chronicles of war, I will take up my slender reed and practise the music of the countryside' (tr. E. V. Rieu). Though he claims not to blush for dwelling in the woods, there is at least postulated the possibility of a return to the world of men. That return occurs by stages and with almost programmatic precision in the succession to the lyrical pastorals of the didactic *Georgics* and the epic *Aeneid*. There is evidence that though Virgil declared himself content with the thin tones of the reed in the *Eclogues*, he later grew increasingly aware of his poetic career as possessing a distinct pattern for which pastoral contemplation provided the initial movement. The very last lines of the *Georgics*, in which Virgil remembers himself in his own words as the singer of Tityrus, are a kind of signature to mark the conclusion of a second stage of his career. And the *Aeneid* itself, in the Middle Ages and the Renaissance, used to be headed by a paragraph, now omitted as probably spurious, to the effect that the poet who once sang of shepherds had exchanged reed for the trumpet. It was directly imitated by Spenser in the first stanza of the Proem to Book I of *The Faerie Queene*.

The view of pastoral, from Virgil's time onwards, is generally an ambivalent one: as symbolizing the life of retirement and leisure apart from the lust for gain and place which characterizes the city, the pastoral world is a beneficent refuge; its narrow bounds represent the circumscription of desire, its simplicity is a welcome relief from the press of affairs in the great world. But because of its country associations, pastoral is also, on the poetic scale, and largely through Virgil's example and conspicuous success as an epic poet, the least of the poetic Kinds, the first step of a ladder with many rungs. In his *Defence of Poesy*, Sidney referred to it as a lowly stile which all could creep over with ease, and Drayton begins one of his eclogues, the fourth, with a similar 'Shepheards, why creepe we in this lowly vaine?' Further, though poetry is essentially a contemplative and not a practical art, and hence retirement and withdrawal are perfectly suitable to the poet, his withdrawal from human affairs may not be so complete as to estrange him from the common world of men and their daily experiences. The complexities inherent in this state of affairs will be developed in the next chapter. For the moment, we must consider in what the value of an entrance into Arcadia consists. As regards the poet, it represents a motion towards self-discovery by way of discipline. It is equivalent to climbing a prospect – a prospect, in this case, surrounded by grander mountains – to see the lie of the land before one undertakes to journey. The poet comes to Arcadia for a clarification of his artistic, intellectual and moral purpose. The assumption of the shepherd's weeds signalizes for a millennium and more a commitment to poetry and to the exploration of the relative worths of the active and contemplative existences. The temporary retirement to the interior landscape becomes a preparation for engagement with the world of reality, for it is necessary for knowledge to precede action. In this connection, it is notable that Aeneas himself follows a similar course; he makes a contemplative descent into the underworld as preparation for a life of active endeavour in Italy as warrior, ruler and (presumably, were the poem completed) husband. Both for princes and poets, an engagement in the active life is a necessity to which they are born, and they are all contemplatives by virtue of that necessity.

Arcadia slept for a thousand years before Sannazaro rediscovered it, in his work by that name, in the early years of the sixteenth century. His *Arcadia* is the first European work to choose as its setting the landscape discovered by Virgil. A mixture of prose and verse, Arcadia is the creation of a lover (Sincero, Sannazaro himself) plunged into grief for the unattainability of his love, and it represents a landscape of withdrawal which, by way of recompense, is a paradise of poetry. It rings constantly, in the songs of the shepherds who inhabit it, with the great pastoral verse of the ancients, here revivified in a vernacular tongue. The *Arcadia* establishes a mood far more than it tells a coherent story, it is characterized by the same interiority that we find in Virgil, and, as in Virgil, its subjects are love, death and poetry. The slightness of the narrative interest is perhaps intended; what is important is the way in which a Petrarchan pastoral of disappointed love finding joy in solitude, along with the gradual and half-unconscious development of poetic powers, is interfused with motifs from the classical pastoral. As Professor Kalstone has shown (pp. 9–39), the move to Arcadia symbolizes a new life for the poet, a prospect opens before him of a radiant future. The situation in which the poet finds himself is as paradoxical as the unreal reality and distant nearness of Arcadia itself: he is a sophisticate among simple men, seeking for himself while he is at every moment giving evidence of having already found himself, losing his originality in order to find it, an unhappy lover in process of becoming (and for that very reason) a great poet. Loss leads in every way to gain. He comes to Arcadia in search of recreation, and in both of its senses. He arrives in search of idyllic peace, for leisure, and for the easing of a burden of grief. But he comes also as a man who cannot change his soul as he changes his sky: his function in Arcadia – and he would not have come there unless he were a poet already; to arrive there at all must be to have possessed it already – is to recreate the past glories of art in his own terms. It is here that he is to explore his commitment to the arts of poetry and to the art of love in its widest sense: it is a place of witness. If he has genius (and that is the possibility he is exploring) he will emerge as the inheritor of a great tradition of poetry thereby earning the right to be himself considered a model of that tradition by poets in future times. Arcadia is then, finally, the place where for purposes of initiation and self-discovery, the Individual Talent is brought into confrontation with the Tradition.

Sannazaro's self-consciousness in this pastoral milieu is even greater than Virgil's, for the grand fact of Virgil's epic achievement is always before the eyes of the Renaissance poet. This self-consciousness introduces a note of ambivalence towards the pastoral setting. Most often it is a place of glorious and sensuous beauty, seen either in a noontide blaze of light or by the soft glamour of the moon. Still, there is sometimes a startling sense of its limitations, voiced most obviously in the Seventh Prose (Nash, p. 72): Sincero tells the shepherds he frequently calls to mind the pleasures of his homeland 'among these Arcadian solitudes in which – by your leave I will say it – I can hardly believe that the beasts of the woodland can dwell with any pleasure, to say nothing of young men nurtured in noble cities.' The usual preference for a world of Nature over Art is here reversed in a moment, a prophecy of later developments to which we have already alluded. Directly connected with this preference for activity in the great world over contemplation in the pastoral world is the idea, several times expressed, that the pastoral is merely the prelude to a greater poetic undertaking. The shepherd Carino bestows a pipe upon Sincero for his singing with the trust that he will in the future 'sing in loftier vein the loves of the Fauns and Nymphs. And even as up to this point you have fruitlessly spent the beginnings of your adolescence among the simple and rustic songs of shepherds, so hereafter you will pass your fortunate young manhood among the sounding trumpets of the most famous poets of your country, not without hope of eternal fame' (Nash, pp. 74–5). Later, in a section where Sannazaro rehearses the entire history of pastoral poetry, from Pan to Theocritus and Virgil and by implication to himself, he notes that Virgil did not content himself with so humble a strain but 'set himself to instruct the rustic tillers of the soil, perhaps with a hope of later singing with more sonorous trumpet the arms of Trojan Aeneas . . .' (Nash, p. 105). Finally, in the epilogue to the work, he urges his instrument not to be heard among courts and palaces, but to remain in its wonted solitudes: 'Your humble sound would ill be heard amid that of the fearsome cornets or the royal trumpets' (Nash, p. 151). Gradually but increasingly as the work nears its end, the décor of epic begins to penetrate the pastures of Arcadia, first by brief allusions, then by open recreation of motifs and scenes from classical epics: the *descensus inferi* of the latter books is the most extended example and probably represents, as it does in the allegorized Virgil, a descent for illumination and spiritual rediscovery.

It would be natural to turn to yet another work bearing the name of *Arcadia* at this point, but we are concerned at the moment with the attitudes of poets towards Arcadias in which they figure personally, and Sidney's masterpiece is concerned with a group of aristocrats in flight from the world of outer reality. That situation initiates a whole series of complexities which are only incipient in Sannazaro. The conflict between Nature and Art, contemplation and activity, pastoral and epic arises in its fullest expression when pastoral becomes conscious of itself as a genre subservient to other genres; when it is brought into amalgamation with them, there is a correspondent raising of the tensions involved. Here, poets who arrive in Arcadia either alone or attended by a very few of their friends, are in search of a solution to their literary problems. They are only the harbingers of a later invasion of courtiers and princes who bear the multiple responsibilities of rule and for whom a pastoral retirement is a matter of great and momentous and sometimes perilous concern.

Sannazaro introduces us to the situation of a despairing lover who, in withdrawal from grief in love, finds himself a poet in recompense. It is not strange therefore to find a constant thread of allusion, in his pastoral poetry and in that of his successors, to myths of unhappy lovers who were also connected with the origins of poetry: to Orpheus, who by the power of his poetry communicated a sympathetic spirit to even inanimate nature; to Pan, who pursued the nymph Syrinx in a love-chase and found her converted into a reed from which he drew the first pastorals; to Apollo who similarly pursued the chaste Daphne, metamorphosed into a laurel-tree whose leaves, woven into a crown, symbolize poetic achievement under the aegis of the god of poetry. Disappointed lovers, gods or humans, become either patrons of poetry or poets themselves.

The condition of being disappointed in love is never uncommon; indeed, if the disappointment is not really experienced, Renaissance poets are perfectly capable of inventing an unhappy situation as the basis of their melancholy. That, apparently, is the situation in *The Shepheardes Calender*. It may seem strange to designate the work as an Arcadian poem; its setting is that of north-eastern Lancashire, Arcadia itself is never mentioned in the course of the poem, and its shepherds are not classical Tityruses or Sinceros, but homely and unprepossessing Hobbinols, Diggons and Colin Clouts. Yet the physical setting is in no way insisted upon, and it becomes obvious that this is Arcadia in a form that is mere English. Pastoral constantly strives to acclimatize and domesticate the distant vision; in so doing, it finds the universal in the particular and gives to the world of daily experience the luminosity of the ideal. Moreover, it is possible for a work not set specifically in the original Arcadia to be infinitely more Arcadian in spirit than one which, like Sidney's *Arcadia*, is. Arcadia is perpetually being renewed because the longing for it is rooted in one of the deepest instincts of man; common to all peoples and all times, it will of necessity wear a different look in different times and places. The attempt to render the distant vision proximate is visible not only in Spenser but also in his contemporaries and followers. In Ben Jonson's exquisite masque, *The Sad Shepherd*, the pastures and shepherds of Arcadia are exchanged quite deliberately for a setting and fable nearer home, Sherwood Forest and the company of Robin Hood. In another masque, Milton's *Arcades*, the Arcadian shepherds are represented as having made a northward journey from their old haunts to a new home in England, a movement that Milton interprets, as John Wallace has shown, not only in artistic but in moral and intellectual terms as well: from a profane to a religious setting, from a world of paganism to a world of Christianity.

Spenser is the first English poet to reinvigorate the Arcadian tradition and his poem reveals both a continuity of the tradition and a sense of novelty that gives him the right to be considered with the ancients themselves. In general, Spenser perpetuates the tradition by writing semi-dramatic eclogues which have as their main subjects, love, death and poetry. On the other hand, his originality appears in some novel and striking conceptions. Where Sannazaro for his own purposes had introduced a newness into pastoral by combining Petrarchan motifs with Virgilian resonances in a form of mixed prose and verse reminiscent of Dante's *Vita Nuova*, Spenser shows his capacity for inventiveness in a wonderfully suitable calendrical scheme that mirrors the progress of a pastoral year. The interpenetration of man and nature which is a constant theme of pastoral is thereby allowed full expression, for the changing seasons of the year are metaphors for the progress of human life from its spring to its winter. Moreover, the calendrical scheme identifies this Arcadia as a world which is fallen and subject to the constant mutations of time. Disappointed love leads to the breaking the shepherd's pipe in a fit of peevishness ('January'), there is uncertainty about the power of poetry to be of any avail against the hard facts of life ('October'), death appears to conquer the young and the beautiful ('November'), and there is tribulation and disorder in the Church ('May', 'July' and 'September').

In the last three eclogues, Spenser demonstrates, like Virgil before him, a disturbing sense of great stirrings in the outer world of reality, and the mood of his northern Arcadia darkens correspondingly. The same darkening effect is produced by thoughts of unhappy love and the apparent uselessness of poetry. Some elemental concerns of humankind have been imported into the supposedly mindless atmosphere of Arcadia, and it is their resolution with which the poet is concerned. In resolving its own dilemma, poetry resolves the other two problems. Disappointment in love has the paradoxical effect of turning the lover into a poet; the apparent uselessness of poetry is seen to be an illusion: it can move men by taking on a different set of tones and providing a national vision that will move men to virtue. The 'October' eclogue is the focus of all these concerns, and there the way is pointed to the epic and to the poetry therefore of the active life. The argument of *The Shepheardes Calender*, it has been well said by Professor Hamilton, is 'the rejection of the pastoral life for the truly dedicated life in the world. For Spenser, this life is that of the heroic poet whose high religious calling is to serve the Queen by inspiring her people to all virtuous action' (p. 181). Once again, therefore, the pastoral place is the place of a vision. In losing his identity in that of Colin Clout, the poet has really found it.

The Arcadian pastoral of pure contentment is almost never the greatest and most serious pastoral art. Drayton and Herrick, with their free range of fancy and their general ignoring of the great issues to which pastoral gives rise in its most ambitious moments, are saved from prettiness by their irony and wit, and yet we sense that an entire world of human concerns is missing from their poems, for which the substitution of great lyric beauty is only a moderate recompense. After Spenser, only Milton and Marvell employ the pastoral withdrawal with an awareness of its high function as an illuminating experience and a sense of its many complexities. Indeed, most of Spenser's followers make of pastoral a mere manner or decorative element.

A revival of the Arcadian eclogue in the days shortly before pastoral was to fall into its degeneracy occurs in the *Pastorals* of Pope, and to read them is to realize how completely an entire world of human issues has fled pastoral to find expression in other forms. This is not to derogate from their great elegance and beauty, nor from their originality, which consists mainly in Pope's cunning selection of themes from the old eclogues and his arrangement of them into a unit of which the basis is the four seasons. He tells us in his 'Preface' to the work that he admired Spenser's calendrical scheme, and his search for originality leads him into the only reduction possible from such a scheme, from twelve months to four seasons. A tendency to standardization is visible not only in the metre of all four, which is that of rhyming pentameter couplets, but also in his very precise selection of themes and forms from the classical pastoral. Thus, Spring is an amoebean contest; Summer, a love complaint; Autumn, a contest which consists of two juxtaposed complaints; and Winter, an elegy. The neatness, simplicity and variety achieved in so limited an area are admirable, but this Arcadia is an Arcadia viewed from the outside; the poet reveals no capacity to enter into an imaginative sympathy with the shepherds he describes, and there is no possibility of his conceiving of himself as one of them. What we miss finally in Pope's pastorals is not only the sense of new beginnings, but also and more importantly, the sense of preparation. The poems take a one-sided view of rural life, and therefore we have its tranquillity rendered with no apparent awareness of the other side of things. The preconceptions that dictated Pope's attitude towards pastoral are best demonstrated from the 'Discourse on Pastoral' with which he prefaced his poems: he tells us there that:

> The original of Poetry is ascribed to that Age which succeeded the creation of the world: and as the keeping of flocks seems to have been the first employment of mankind, the most ancient sort of poetry was probably *pastoral*. It is natural to imagine, that the leisure of those ancient shepherds admitting and inviting some diversion, none was so proper to that solitary and sedentary life as singing; and that in their songs they took occasion to celebrate their own felicity.

As we have been attempting to show, perfect felicity is never the subject of pastoral when it is truly serious, and complacency is not the feeling from which it arises. Nor is pastoral poetry the creation of shepherds themselves; it requires another perspective entirely. Besides, we know what ordinarily happens when simple people, not necessarily shepherds but close enough, are discovered to have a bent for poetry. They do not sing their own felicity. The latter eighteenth century discovered at various times poetical threshers, milkmaids and shoemakers, and their entire ambition was to desert their rude station as quickly as possible and write in the sophisticated style of the day. As Professor Tinker's splendid little volume shows, the fate of these unfortunates (Stephen Duck, Ann Yearsley or 'Lactilla', and James Woodhouse) was always melancholy when it was not, as in the case of the last, horrific and grim.

The views on pastoral that Pope voices are those of the academies, particularly those of the French academies, as Professor Congleton has shown in a survey of later attitudes to pastoral. Critics like Rapin and Fontenelle had decided the laws of the form, categorized its possible subjects, determined its origin. When Pope writes in his 'Discourse' that 'We must therefore use some illusion to render a Pastoral delightful; and this consists in exposing the best side only of a shepherd's life, and in concealing its miseries' he is merely repeating a common position. That the position itself has not the slightest relation to the issues of pastoral as we have been watching them in their development, works finally to the detriment of his own pastoral art. For him, as for his age, the whole question of pastoral existence was reduced to a delightful game. As such it survived for a while, but having no inside, so to speak, it crumbled easily before the onslaughts of the succeeding age. Johnson on 'Lycidas' and Goldsmith on unutterably more trivial pieces (in 'Letter CVI' of *The Citizen of the World*) are two voices raised up in disgust at the folly of the academic pastoral, though the latter surely has more justice on his side than the former. And perhaps Congreve's Lady Wishfort, when her world is in danger of collapsing, voices the feeling of the century towards pastoral as the absolute dead-end: 'Well, friend, you are enough to reconcile me to the bad world, or else I would retire to deserts and solitudes; and feed harmless sheep by groves and purling streams. Dear Marwood, let us leave the world, and retire by ourselves and be shepherdesses' (*The Way of the World*, V). If pastoral had long passed into satire, so too had the epic. The age proved incapable of both.

In spite of external changes, which were only a testimony to the way in which poets were able to reinvigorate an old ideal in their own terms, the myth of Arcadia functioned for over a millennium and a half as a repository of human ideals. For manifold reasons, of which the chiefest is the *real* return to nature which effectually silenced all the voices of pastoral, the image of Arcadia ceased to function in the eighteenth century, and in that form has never been resuscitated. This is not to say, however, that a version of Arcadia is not yet with us and likely to remain with us as long as humans aspire to simplicity. But the task of any modern author who endeavours to project his aspiration into a landscape is immeasurably more difficult, because his situation is wholly unlike that of poets previous to the eighteenth century. The latter could invoke the Arcadian ideal with ease; it was universal, a common heritage for any European artist with the slightest acquaintance with the tradition. The very accessibility of Arcadia led inevitably to a good deal of nonsense, but, frequently enough to justify its existence, to works of genius and splendour. The case of the modern author is complicated by the fact that there is no common myth to which he can appeal for a pastoral art; in effect, he is forced back upon his own imagination for the creation of such a myth. Most likely, he will attempt to create it from a real landscape with which he is familiar, from a set of local circumstances that have coloured his vision.

The truth of that remark has been recently demonstrated by Maynard Mack in his book on Pope in his country retreat at Twickenham. Here, at the very point in time when the old Arcadian ideal has withered and failed, a new ideal is created from a particular local environment by an act of the mythopoeic imagination. Landscape becomes both actual and symbolic, and the central figure within it, the poet himself, becomes both the actual man and an heroic figure in what Mack terms 'a highly traditional confrontation between virtuous simplicity and sophisticated corruption' (p. 8). This picture of rural contentment is perhaps more Horatian than Virgilian, rural rather than pastoral, but there are enough Virgilian resonances – particularly in the sense of transporting and acclimatizing the muses of Latium to the banks of the Thames (p. 39) – to show the direction that Pope's mind was taking. The new Arcadias will inevitably participate in the old, though they are more localized. Those who follow in the tradition of Arcadian pastoral will inevitably recapitulate Pope's process of moving from the particular to the general, from the local and realistic to the universal and symbolic. Hence, writers like Hardy, Housman or Frost are invariably associated with a particular landscape – South-western England, Shropshire, New Hampshire – in contrast to the old pastoralists who were associated with no such place, even when they viewed Arcadia through their own native landscapes. Who would think of Spenser or Jonson as a regionalist in any way? The peculiar value of Arcadia is that it never existed. It was, from its very first appearance, a literary creation, a projection of the mind, and therefore a universal. The old poets could invoke it as such, infusing into its description as much or as little of their own surroundings to acclimatize and domesticate an ideal that remained essentially itself.

In contrast, the modern author begins from a particular environment and attempts, by an artful selection of detail, to render the particular a universal. Wessex, Shropshire and New Hampshire are ultimately all places of the mind, as well as places rooted in geographical reality. They do not represent renderings of actual reality because there is no reason to render them with photographic precision. In every case there is a choice of detail which reveals a prescinding from reality as clear as that which distinguishes Arcadia. It is detail, however, of so individual a nature that we may not recognize it as the product of selection at all. If we avoid this error and see the creation as essentially one of the imagination, an internal world projected into a familiar landscape and utilizing all the values of that particular environment but ordering them as reality is never ordered, we may come to a realization of the difficulties inherent in such a creative act. In effect the modern author creates his own cosmos, a world personal and individual that demands attention in its own right and seeks also to be admitted as a universal. His Arcadia recapitulates his entire intellectual life, but however private and personal it may be, it has claims upon general humanity. A modern Arcadia is bound to be a witness to the spiritual fragmentation of the Western world, no less than the systems which Joyce or Yeats attempt to erect from their own private experience to give coherence to their vision. The process of criticism in dealing with such a self-generated world is immeasurably more difficult than it was in the days of the original Arcadia; the problem of belief is even greater. The glory of the olden realm of Arcadia was that it unified belief and a tradition of poetry as well.

4
The Nearness of Sparta

The entrance in the Renaissance of figures other than poets into the fastnesses of Arcadia is the occasion for pastoral to break out of its normal classical and medieval forms, the eclogue and the lyric, and to assume the more complex forms of the drama and the epic. A correspondent complexity appears in the issues to which this movement gives birth, for if it is right and proper for poets to enter this land of retirement and contemplation, it may not be wholly so for the great and the near-great whose sphere is the world of active endeavour. The confrontation of two worlds, contemplative and active, is mirrored in the confrontation of two classes of people, shepherds and courtiers, and yet again in the kinds of poetry proper to each, pastoral and epic.

Curiously, the first great epic of the Western world springs from the unfortunate action of a royal figure who was once a shepherd. Paris was sent at birth to be a shepherd in the hills by his fearful mother, to whom an oracle had revealed that he was to be a source of destruction; the wrong choice he made between the goddesses Venus, Juno and Minerva proved the correctness of the prophecy. From the first, therefore, epic and pastoral are inextricably connected, and the capacity of pastoral leisure to lead away from contemplative values is amply suggested by Paris's choice. The simple green world may be a place of disorder as well as recreation, and we may only return to it if we are aware of what once happened there, to Paris as well as to Adam. It is not a panacea for every malady.

The myth of Paris was allegorized at an early time in the Middle Ages, as Professor Smith has shown (pp. 3–9), and to the goddesses who appeared to him were ascribed different and symbolic values. Venus represented the life of pleasure and ease and love; Juno, the life of activity, rule, aspiration and heroic ambition; and Minerva, the life of contemplation and wisdom. The myth is beautifully recreated in one of the first pastoral plays in England, George Peele's *The Arraignment of Paris*.

The myth establishes an obvious hierarchy of values. The feral life of the senses is subordinated to the life of virtuous activity in the world, and both to the life of the mind embodied in Minerva. That is, in general, the traditional and orthodox view of both the Middle Ages and the Renaissance, though in the latter period a complication results from the newly emphasized value accorded to the active life. Where Dante's pilgrimage culminates in a vision of the celestial city, the great epics of the Renaissance culminate in the establishment of an earthly city and the celebration of the life of the world. The chief stress is upon the exercise of virtue in the active life, in the restoration or renewal of a fallen society, and though contemplation is a necessary precondition, it is only through activity that mankind can cleanse his surroundings. Thus, though Bacon associates the contemplative pastoral life with Abel, and the life of activity with the farmer Cain (Smith, p. 3), and thus preserves the hierarchy of contemplation over activity, he qualifies that notion in another place by asserting that 'men must know that in this theatre of man's life it is reserved only for God and the angels to be lookers on . . .' (Greenlaw, p. 148). The same idea finds expression in Milton's *Areopagitica* in the famous lines about fugitive and cloistered virtue that will not enter into the dust and heat of the race when there is a garland to be won. It is dramatized by Spenser in the tenth canto of Book I of *The Faerie Queene* when Redcrosse Knight is directed away from the vision of the Heavenly Jerusalem to resume his quest in the world and so gain it by struggle. And it is again dramatized by Sidney in his masque *The Lady of May*, presented before Queen Elizabeth, and clearly meant to demonstrate the superiority of the active forester over the contemplative shepherd.

It is true, as Professor Smith is at pains to demonstrate, that the pastoral represented for the Renaissance an ideal of *otium* as opposed to *negotium*, of leisure for contemplation and self-restoration which is at the opposite end of the scale from vulgar and avaricious money-grubbing and submission to the vagaries of fortune. But to say that is to play upon the simple contrast of town and country, of Art and Nature, which results in a simple preference for the latter over the former. It is essentially a lyric feeling, and it succumbs easily to the more ruminative consideration that greater forms of literature will give to it. Renaissance authors were generally aware of a greater tension in the complex of ideas. Even the elements in the hierarchy of which we spoke a moment ago are capable of subtle distinctions which may alter the perspective. Thus, for example, the impulse to pleasure presided over by Venus has a dual potentiality: it can work beneficently, towards procreation and replenishment of the race, and maliciously, towards self-indulgence and lust. The active life presided over by Juno may operate in the same dual way: it can involve an exercise of power for legitimate gain and for the heroic achievement of justice, or, perverted, it can lead to avariciousness and tyranny. Even the contemplative life is capable of this duality: retirement from the world may symbolize a desire for contemplation and a lack of aspiration that is virtuous; but it may also be an indication of forgetfulness of high purpose, a dropping out of the race when the garland is yet to be won. In that light, it is capable of being a retirement into sloth. Heroic purpose can yield to desire for leisure, leisure can lead to a yearning for amorous delight. After all, Oiseuse or Idleness is the portress to the garden of delight in the *Roman de la Rose*, and Ease introduces the masque of Cupid in *The Faerie Queene* (III, xii).

It is against this background that the courtiers from the ravaged

E

realms bordering on Arcadia enter the pastoral setting, propelled either by chance or by their own intention. The first intrusion into the pastoral world of delight and innocence by the chivalric world of quest and heroic purpose occurs in medieval literature, in the *pastourelle* as we saw earlier, and it was evident there that for the knights who came the great delight of the green world lay wholly in its providing an arena for love. The knights of the *pastourelle* herald the coming, by many and various means, of the large numbers of knights and ladies, kings and princesses and courtiers, who invade the pastoral world in the works of the dramatic and epic poets of the Renaissance. Either they come in their own persons (as in Shakespeare, Sidney, Spenser and Ariosto) and they then co-exist with the shepherds and shepherdesses of Arcadia in a state of ambiguous harmony; or (as in Tasso, Guarini and Fletcher) they take on the guise of the shepherds and shepherdesses themselves, and then it is their values, their interests, their manners and morals, which become the main focus of interest. One need no longer be a poet to gain entrance into Arcadia; to be an aristocrat is more than sufficient.

As the original inhabitants of Arcadia are gradually displaced by the courtly invaders, they frequently undergo a curious change. We have already seen that Sannazaro had a moment of doubt about the supposed loveliness of their rustic lives, and this note is increasingly explored until it results in pure burlesque of the rural existence. In Sidney's *Arcadia*, for example, the shepherd family of Damoetas, Miso and Mopsa who are set over King Basileus's daughters as guardians, are as repellent as their antecedents were lovely, or at least picturesque. The daughter, Mopsa, is accorded a mock blazon of her beauties in chapter III of Book I ('*Like great god* Saturn *faire, and like faire* Venus *chaste*') and Damoetas himself is singularly missing in that one element that distinguished the shepherds of the past, a native courtliness of manner. In Greene's *Menaphon* Carmela is told that she has lips like cucumbers, and that her breath is 'like the steam of apple pies'. And in Shakespeare's *As You Like It*, Audrey and William are *par excellence* the types of thick-witted rusticity, counter-balanced, on the other hand, by two other figures who represent the shepherd and shepherdess in their more idealized form, Phoebe and Silvius.

This conscious awareness of the double nature of shepherd life is most fully expressed in Sidney's *Arcadia*. The Damoetas family is only one side of the picture of the pastoral existence in the work, and it is balanced by the descriptions, occurring at the end of each book, of the activities of more idealized shepherds also residing in that country. Into the eclogues and dances of these true Arcadians Sidney infuses a Neoplatonic view of love and life that acts as a polar star to the erratic actions of the royal party. There is a spirituality, therefore, in Arcadian life that co-exists with coarseness and unuplifted crudity by which it remains untouched, and in this aspect Arcadia is only a mirror of the greater world, containing within itself both perfection and imperfection, idealism and coarse reality.

The artfulness of certain shepherds in Renaissance pastoral is sometimes explicable in other terms, and here again we have a complication. In Tasso's *Jerusalem Delivered*, in Guarini's *Pastor Fido*, in Spenser's *The Faerie Queene*, in Shakespeare's *Cymbeline*, we note the presence of a shepherd who has reversed the normal order of things and has fled from the country to the court, returning in disgust and dissatisfaction to the contentedness of his original lowly station. The process is thus Nature-Art-Nature and it reverses the course appropriate to the courtiers, which is that of Art-Nature-Art. For the shepherd to return to Arcadia is for him to find a milieu which is wholly appropriate to him; he is a model of deliberately contracted ambitions and circumscribed desires, and we can measure the corruption of the world of Art by his plain-spoken and sincere condemnations. This preference for country ways and manners is rooted in the simple rather than the complex view of rural life, but it is given an additional twist of complexity by being put into the mouth of a shepherd who has seen both sides of the question; he has been a townsman and he *knows*. The original of all these shepherds appears to be the Tityrus of Virgil's first eclogue, who in order to be happy at home has had to go to Rome. The experience of both worlds is necessary for happiness.

The experience of these shepherds demonstrates that the courtly invaders should undergo no less simple an experience, and that therefore their flight to the country is not the terminus of their quest. It is expected of the great who rightly flee the tainted world of courtly corruption that they too will have an illuminating experience in the forests, but that ultimately they will return to their own proper sphere, which is the world of Art, the city and the court, and renew and regenerate it by the knowledge they have gained. There is nothing intrinsically good about the country, or intrinsically evil about the town. It is only human waywardness that makes the latter evil. Evil, however, is capable of being turned into good and the motives which led to it are susceptible of redirection. For better or for worse, the town is here to stay, it is a type of social organization that directly results from the Fall, and what we do or fail to do within its confines will determine our destinies. For townsmen arriving in Arcadia, therefore, the hospitality of its groves and pastures is limited and temporary.

The remark just made about the permanence of the town introduces another consideration. There are two contrasting views about the city and the country in Western thought, both dependent upon the views of Nature we have seen in the introduction. We have been dealing so far with the city as a place of corruption and confusion, and with the country as a place of residual wholesomeness and simplicity. The view looks towards Adam's prelapsarian state with envy and longing as an ineffably superior state and desires for ever to recreate it. But there is another side of things. The very word 'civilization', implying all the progress that man has made in his history that separates him from the other creatures of the earth, is tied to the notion that the creation of cities and their societies is what truly marks him off from them. Cities represent an advance from the days when he cohabited with beasts in the forest. The word 'civilization', with its root in the Latin '*civis*' or '*civitas*' contains in essence the notion of a smoothing down of feral instincts, of harmonious co-operation between men in a society which is more elaborate than that in field or cave. This view looks on Adam's postlapsarian state in the forlorn world immediately after the expulsion from the garden as a state ineffably inferior to modern man's, graced as this is by the cultivation of arts and sciences. We would all be happy to enjoy the first bliss of Adam in the garden if we could; since we cannot, and since the creation of cities is a testimony to both our fall and our possible rise, we must strive continually to make them as paradisal as we can through the disciplines of law and of reason. Adam's experience initiates the typical Christian pattern of fall and ascent. Our experience of the city recapitulates his fall in the garden, but the world itself may be made the place in which we recover, not the first, but a higher innocence, and an innocence gained through experience.

Some of the greatest masterpieces of our literature re-enact this progression from the garden to the city and hold this double view of the latter as a phenomenon resulting directly from the Fall but also as an example of man's creativity and therefore of his capacity to regenerate himself. *The Divine Comedy*, the *Orlando Furioso*, *The Faerie Queene*, and *Comus* all begin in a forest haunted by the outbreak of animal passion; in various ways, they all move to the creation of the city as emblematic of man's capacity to work out the beast in his nature and to achieve a state of interior harmony. Those cities will inevitably be corrupted by human passion and ambition, and another flight to the forest will take place. The process of flight and return is continuous, and it will endure till the death of the race.

The return, then, is the important thing: pastoral retirement is not an end in itself. All of Shakespeare's pastoral plays, for example, terminate in a return to the court. There are only two instances (both in *As You Like It*) of a refusal to do so, and they are the exception that proves the rule. It is clear that Touchstone remains behind in Arden because he finds the delights of the country embodied in the sluttish sensuality of Audrey too strong a call upon his nature to resist. Jacques remains because the forest provides a setting for another kind of self-indulgence, which is that of melancholy: his is what Poggioli calls the 'pastoral of the self'. Both prefer to stand outside the re-established harmony of the social order, an order for which the central metaphor is the series of marriages between the various parties of country and court.

Not only is the pastoral world not a panacea for every ill, it is capable of providing the impulse to disaster very directly, as well as restoring the vision that leads to renewal. It depends ultimately on the reasons for which one has come to it, the predisposition of the heart and brain. Three pastoral cases in Tasso, Ariosto and Spenser will illustrate the different ways in which the pastoral retreat is considered.

In *Jerusalem Delivered*, Erminia is in love with Tancredi, who in turn is in love with the pagan warrior Clorinda. Drawn by love of a man who is completely unaware of her existence, Erminia disguises herself in Clorinda's armour in an attempt to reach the Christian camp and cure his battle wounds. The passage in which she debates with herself on this perilous course of action (VI, 70–8) introduces an elaborate psychomachia between Honour and Love, won, of course, by the latter. Her night-time expedition nearly ends in disaster, as she is mistaken by the vigilant Christians for Clorinda, and as a consequence the heroine is driven to flight, a flight that takes her, purely by chance, into a pastoral setting (VII, 1–22). She arrives at a time of crisis in her existence, and the courtly sophistications of her world of warfare and love find a strange contrast in the simple pastoral world. The impoverished but happy shepherd who relieves her had once been a member of the great world, and he had fled from the troubles of the court to the untroubled joys of his early pastoral life.

The pastoral oasis here functions as a pointed contrast to the fortune-ridden world of love and strife which is the main setting of the poem's action. Erminia's is what Poggioli calls a pastoral of innocence, a pastoral in which the economic and social values of the golden age are asserted, and from which the emphasis on libertine love which provides the basis for the 'pastoral of happiness' is wholly absent. The contraction of social ambitions represented by the shepherd's deliberate withdrawal from the court finds an analogue in the similarly contracted scope of Erminia's love. As he finds happiness by accepting his fate in a lowly setting, she likewise withdraws from the great world of splendid and heroic love into a more intimate sphere of her own, nourishing her love and recognizing the impossibility of its achievement. That is why she enters so naturally into the pastoral setting, arraying herself as a shepherdess and performing the simple actions appropriate to her simple station. Tancredi is never to be hers; he belongs for ever to the Clorinda whom he assaults and kills by error and then baptizes. Later in the poem, in curing him when he is on the point of death (XIX, 103–14) and then vanishing out of his existence, Erminia finds her happiness, as the shepherd finds his, within herself alone. Not for everyone is the glamorous life on the lofty stages of the world, and the ways to felicity are many and various.

Both pastorals are present in Ariosto's *Orlando Furioso*, and in a more sophisticated form than in Tasso. One of the main threads of the poem concerns itself with the love-pursuit by Charlemagne's paladin Orlando of the pagan enchantress, Angelica. The latter's function as a symbol of a hapless instigation to lust and disorder is revealed at the very beginning of the poem (I, 35 ff.) where she is discovered in a *locus amoenus* where one of her many lovers sings disconsolately of the flowering and death of the rose of virginity, and of the need for its timely plucking while it is still a bud. The note of *carpe diem* is sounded again in the eighth canto (71 ff.) where a troubled Orlando muses by night upon the 'flower' that he fears will be for ever lost to him if Angelica should have yielded to any other. His ensuing dream about wandering in a flowering landscape of love and enjoying the highest felicity of consummation turns immediately into a nightmare in which the garden is destroyed by the fury of a sudden tempest that devastates the flowers and leaves him in an agony of frustrated desire. The vision initiates his departure from a beleaguered Paris of which he is the strongest arm, and culminates in the twenty-third canto, the exact centre of the poem, in which the madness arising from the sexual frustration overtakes the paladin in a climax of astonishing psychological power. The pastoral setting in which the paladin loses the last vestiges of a reason that he has so plentifully abused is directly related to the two passages to which we have just alluded: all three are concerned, explicitly, with the gathering of roses, and it is fitting therefore that the madness which is the punishment for the abuse of his reason should overtake Orlando in a place traditionally associated with the liberation of 'pure' instinct. In the very place to which Orlando comes in this central canto, Angelica and her lover Medoro had come earlier (XIX) and there the simple young soldier had, by a rapid whirl of the inconstant wheel of madcap-fortune, been allowed to set foot into the 'garden' and to pluck the 'rose' that so many had sought in vain before him: Ariosto is very explicit in his imagery. The shepherd family that receives these two refugees from the great world into its humble cottage looks with benign complacency upon the flowering of this ambiguous love; we hear nothing about the usual pastoral contentment here, nothing about pastoral innocence, and indeed the shepherd's wife is happy to stand as a ludicrous matron of honour in a mock marriage ceremony for which Ariosto mischievously says *Amore* was the '*auspice*' or 'best man'. This is the darker side of the pastoral life, and Ariosto etches it with deliberate irony. The instinct no sooner arises than it is satisfied, and the very trees into which the two lovers carve the memories of their raptures (XIX, 36) become favourable witnesses of their joy. The pastoral of happiness has never been so cunningly dramatized as in this pastoral interlude in the midst of a raging world of war.

Those very trees, those grottoes, caves and fountains which memorialize the loves of Angelica and Medoro are for the disappointed Orlando symbols of the ultimate horror of his own sensual frustration. In the central canto, the destruction that they undergo at his hands as he shatters them in the tempestuous outbreak of his passions and the engulfing of his reason by madness, is the most dramatic rendition in literature of what the yearning or pastoral contentment of this kind can do to the fragile sovereignty of reason over desire. With shattering and perfect fitness, the destruction of the pastoral place (of which the paladin once dreamed, it may be recalled) is succeeded by a grimly hilarious destruction of its inhabitants, brought by all the uproar to come running in an evil hour. The garden, once before destroyed in a prophetic dream, is now destroyed again in fact: the destruction is an inevitability, for it is only a human illusion. It is of its essence that it cannot survive, for it seeks only to perpetuate the moment. In the visitation of Orlando's fury upon the place, the shepherds and ultimately himself, we see a furious turning upon the notion of pastoral liberation for the enjoyment of love in an atmosphere of 'wanton innocence'. The pastoral of happiness is always overshadowed by a consideration that it is only a refuge from reality that must eventually be faced: that is what accounts for the melancholy which overlay its description in Tasso's golden age chorus from *Aminta*, and that is what accounts for this more pointed annihilation of its brief splendours in Ariosto.

Orlando's quest for Angelica terminates in a garden, and madness in a pastoral retreat that reflects his inner yearnings is the inevitable result. But though he gives his name to the poem, Orlando is subordinate to yet another hero who is the dynastic hero of the poem and from whose loins the race of the d'Estes of Ferrara, Ariosto's patrons, are eventually to spring. Ruggiero's course of action in the poem, which is largely an evasion of his great destiny, terminates in a providential shipwreck that deposits him unscathed on an island, the refuge of a virtuous old hermit who instructs him in his destiny and finally baptizes him. Like Orlando, Ruggiero arrives at a place presided over by simplicity in love, but the spuriousness of the one is a testimony to the genuineness of the other. The hale and hearty old hermit, who regenerates Ruggiero in body and soul and lives prosperously and abstemiously upon water and fruit supplied by the trees, is a type of the true 'pastor' and his function is one of correction and instruction rather than of complacency in evil. His confrontation with this life of retired simplicity leads to a contemplative experience for the beleaguered hero, and the course of his destiny lies open before him. The pastoral place is therefore, for both Orlando and Ruggiero, the place of a vision. In the one case, the vision deprives Orlando of a reason that he had constantly abused with the fictions of love. In the other case, the vision appears in a recognition of destiny and a willingness to undertake it, and it leads to marriage, the achievement of a kingdom, and an entrance into the active life as warrior, husband and dynast.

Orlando's devastation of the pastoral world is a witness of how utterly fragile it is in the face of an assault from without. The same sense of its vulnerability emerges in the pastoral cantos of Book VI of *The Faerie Queene*. Calidore, the knight of courtesy, happens, in his heroic quest in pursuit of the Blatant Beast, into a pastoral world of exquisite loveliness and simplicity, and his love for the shepherdess Pastorella leads him into an enjoyment of rural society that leads climactically to a vision of the Graces and to the resumption of his quest. What appears to be a desertion of duty is really an illumination of purpose, and the terms in which his vision is conceived shed light upon the idea of retirement as it affects humans marked out for different destinies and pursuing different ways to achieve them. We have been concerned to show how Arcadia is first the realm into which single poets came for purposes of recreation and contemplation, and later the realm invaded or intruded upon by aristocrats in flight from the world. In the tenth canto of Spenser's 'Legend of Courtesy', the poet and the knight are together in the rural landscape. Wandering in the fields one day, Calidore hears the sound of piping and, drawn on by the music, is enchanted by a momentary glimpse of the pastoral poet Colin Clout playing to a hundred naked maidens dancing in a ring in whose centre the three Graces of classical mythology dance about a single maiden of peerless beauty. The Graces are the symbol of that generous giving and receiving which is the essence of the virtue of courtesy, and their dance is representative of that harmonic flow of graciousness from individual to individual which is visible in the world at its elevated best. The poet participates in that motion by a motion of love, his poetry itself, but as soon as the knight appears on the scene, the vision vanishes in an instant and leaves the poet in a misery which all the knight's apologies scarcely serve to alleviate. The dancers dance in naked beauty before the poet who is the only human who gains entrance to this particular landscape; it is proper for him to be in this kind of retirement, for these are haunts known to him since the days of *The Shepheardes Calender*, and he has proven his capacity to engage the great world of heroic action, in the very poem in fact of which the 'Legend of Courtesy' is a part. He enjoys the vision fully and freely. What the knight sees, however, he sees by accident and as an intruder, and his momentary perception of those ideal forms is no more than a glimpse of spiritual beauty of which his quest is but the mirror. He has yet to prove himself by the

achievement of his quest. He cannot enjoy the sight with the freedom of Colin Clout lest the rapture of it withdraw him into a
contemplative retirement which is proper to the artist at this
point, but not to the soldier. The Graces represent a vision of
courtesy that serves as a beacon to illuminate his search for it in
the world. Without that vision, the quest is meaningless.

The fragility of the pastoral vision is again dramatized in
another section, along with the necessity for an active courtesy
that will be mild in reproof of misconduct, but hard in redress of
absolute wrong. At the moment when the Brigants invade the
world of the shepherds (X, 39 ff.), first making them captive and
then slaying them all with the single exception of Pastorella who
miraculously survives, we sense the full brutality of the outer
world and recognize why the vision of the Graces is so brief a
thing. Calidore goes to the rescue of Pastorella in the guise of a
shepherd, but a shepherd who has abandoned his crook and re-
sumed his sword. The resumption and achievement of his quest
follow naturally, but even here there is a sense of an end being
merely a beginning, for the Blatant Beast escapes and must be re-
captured – eternally, Spenser implies. Professor Cheney (p. 238)
puts the matter into its clearest focus:

> It is characteristic of the pastoral mode, as employed by Spenser and
> the poets of the succeeding century, that it sees the pastoral escape as a
> temporary one, at the end of which the civilized shepherd has watched
> his simple 'natural' world lose its innocence and become an exact
> image of his own fallen world, with the same conflicts arising from
> man's mixed nature, and with the same promise of nothing beyond a
> limited and temporary victory in this life.

Before the tragedy of the pastoral massacre, at the point where
Calidore first enters the pastoral world, there occurs a dialogue
which contains an illuminating statement about the pursuit of
happiness. Calidore looks with envy upon the shepherds and expresses the wish that his own fortune could be transposed 'From

pitch of higher place into this low degree' (IX, 28). Meliboee's response is that men accuse the heavens in vain, for they ordain what is best for every man. For each it is fittest that he remain content with what he has: 'It is the mynd that maketh good or ill.' This declaration, especially by one who has made trial of both the country and the court, holds a profound truth, and it sheds an ironic light upon the actions of aristocrats who think to evade their destinies and enjoy a greater bliss by the mere assumption of a pastoral disguise. The passions that assail them in the great world assail them in the green world as well. In entering the pastoral atmosphere, they sometimes attempt to stave off an experience which they must undergo, and which ironically comes upon them through their very attempts to evade it. The pastoral world, sought out as a refuge for the evasion of providential order, frequently reveals how short-sighted and fallible men are, with ironies of the most piercing kind.

Sidney's aristocrats in the *Arcadia* of 1593 provide the best examples. In trying to evade an ambiguous oracle, King Basileus abnegates his royal duties and moves his family off to rustic lodges in the country, thereby setting in motion an entire train of events that prove the oracle right from the first. In trying to escape the order of Providence he falls into an order provided by the vagaries of Fortune. The pastoral world therefore becomes a source of irony, immense complications rising up in the very place which was sought for simplicity.

Irony of another kind rises up in the two princes' attempted evasion of another experience central to human life, that of love. Pyrochles falls in love with one of Basileus's carefully guarded daughters, disguises himself as an Amazon to gain access to her, and arouses the wonderment and irritation of his cousin Musidorus, shortly to fall into the same kind of love-longing for the other of the king's daughters, and to assume only slightly less ignoble a disguise. As he confesses later, his first threatenings, warnings and counsels were offered from no great fund of experience: 'I find indeed, that all is but lip-wisdome, which wants experience.' And again: '. . . . can any man resist his creation? certainly by love we are made, and to love we are made' (*Arcadia*, ed. Feuillerat, I, 113). The pastoral world is the place where one learns that one is not passionless, that to assume that one is, is to assume an innocence about human nature that is not in accord with reality. We are all given a capacity for love which is the common bond of humankind, but that love must be ordered and directed. To attempt to deny it altogether is to fail to realize that, in our fallen condition, experience may be the means of achieving another innocence; just as, for example, our experience in the restored society of the city may be the way of redressing the fall in the garden.

The theme of recovering an innocence in love through experience and not through thoughtless denial of its powers runs through two of the greatest pastoral dramas of the Renaissance, Guarini's *Il Pastor Fido* and Fletcher's *The Faithful Shepherdess*. The shepherds and shepherdesses of these plays are clearly the courtiers of the d'Estes and of James I in a pastoral disguise, and they live constantly above their intellectual means. The Neoplatonic view of love in both dramas results in the display of an entire spectrum of attitudes towards love – animal, human, spiritual – which is personified in the chief characters. The traditional antithesis of Diana and Venus is frequently invoked, and excesses and deficiencies of passion confront each other constantly. The hero of Guarini's play is the young Thessalian hunter Silvio, who addresses himself solely to the hunt of the goddess Diana and scorns the delights of Venus. He is a figure in the mould of the classical Hippolytus or (on a more serious level) of Shakespeare's Adonis; in so far as he has not yet made trial of the thing he scorns, he is an example of deficiency in passion; in so far as he displays an over-enthusiastic fervour for the hunt, he is an example of excess. Ultimately, of course, his sin is one of human pride and self-absorption and, by bringing him to a realization of the potential destructiveness of his passion for hunting, the drama inculcates the notion that the best course is to achieve a union of the best aspects of the goddesses of love and chastity. To deny the experience of love is equivalent to retreating into contemplation without first experiencing the world of human activity; it produces 'lip-wisdome' and a denial of one's fundamental humanity. But Venus and Diana may achieve a harmony, chastity moderating passion, passion moderating chastity. It is the same view that we find expressed in Book III of *The Faerie Queene*, the Legend of married chastity.

The case of the faithful shepherdess who gives her name to Fletcher's play is very much different from that of Silvio. She remains constant to the memory of a great love that has ended in death, and her retirement to solitary contemplation in the forest is made with full awareness of what love is. Her position is taken from the point of view of knowledge and experience, not from ignorance as in the case of Silvio. It is not merely a denial of love, but an exaltation or sublimation of love. Her state of innocence is achieved after experience, his state of innocence consists merely in being as yet untried. The latter is a mere potency whose only virtue, if it is virtue at all, is that it has not determined for good or for evil. Time and the ineluctable workings of Providence, again working through the faulty instrument of the limited and fallacious human will, bring a final illumination to the young hunter. Hence the final chorus can state that 'True joy is a thing/That springs from virtue after suffering' (tr. Sir Richard Fanshawe).

An entrance into the pastoral world represents, then, not an end but a beginning. If anything, the pastoral world is itself a microcosm of the greater world, and it magnifies as under a glass and for our better understanding, the very problems that press in upon us so confusingly there. In so doing, and by considering the whole scope of human activity, pastoral frequently magnifies itself. The initial impulse to pastoral is essentially lyric, and the lyric note persists through the many modifications of the form. In becoming epic and dramatic, pastoral reveals an astonishing power to mount beyond its simple lyric beginnings and to weave itself into the highest forms of all. Indeed, it is capable of creating, in the case of the two works we have just discussed, an entirely new genre, that of pastoral tragicomedy. It is an inescapable irony that a form of literature devoted to counselling humility and simplicity should demonstrate such clear tendencies to aspiration, and in aspiring, achieve so much.

5

The Retreat into Childhood

It has been some time since the pastoral was the province of knights and shepherds, and we should, in the limited space remaining, glance briefly at the child, the figure who more than any other has taken their place and whose connection with pastoral we have already noted in the chapter on the golden age. The pastoral of childhood in the form of the novel is the bequest to us, like the eclogue and the elegy, of antiquity. The association of childhood and pastoral is implicit from the first in the *Idylls* of Theocritus, but the author whom we know by the name of Longus was the first freely and thoroughly to explore the vein of supposed innocence in young people. His romance, *Daphnis and Chloe*, the earliest form of the pastoral novel, had little effect on the great chivalric-pastoral romances of the sixteenth century, largely because they were the result of the fusion of various other literary traditions, but also because the exploration of childhood sensibilities seem to have been of no particular interest to our forebears. Though the décor and cast of the chivalric-pastoral romances is sometimes like that of this earlier purely pastoral romance – pastoralism, foundlings, pirates, providential restorations to wealthy parents – the suggestion might be made that its true descendant is the modern novel of childhood and adolescence. There is no direct influence whatever, and yet the presence in both of certain motifs, especially that of incipient sexuality and of the pleasures it generates, is very striking.

Practically the entire subject of *Daphnis and Chloe* is the awakening of the passion of love in the two foundlings who give their names to the tale. Their ignorance, first of its name and nature, and then of the ways by which it may be consummated, provides the work with its subtle and charming ironies. In many ways, Longus is very like Theocritus in portraying a golden world of youth and beauty, but by the gesture of irony implicit in the complex simplicity of his language, revealing that it is a world that has never been and will never be except in the imagination of an older and wiser human being. Daphnis and Chloe are too simple, too naïvely libertine to be real. Longus paints a world of nature, but it is a world governed at every point by the processes of art. The constant self-awareness of the author extends even to the droll mockery of his own narrative tricks, and his treatment of his hero and heroine maintains an enchanting balance between lyricism and humour. They might have been mere libertines or they might have been mere rustics, but in Longus the two are one. Both the humour and the irony of the work stem from the fact that the unlucky pair of neophytes in sensuality can learn nothing from nature about relief for their predicament, even though they live in surroundings where the natural process is visible at every moment. Even from the mating of goats they can learn nothing, and their awkward attempts at fruition in imitation of those lecherous animals result, curiously, in an augmented sense of their innocence and simplicity. It is a line both dangerous and daring, and it is oddly successful.

The vulnerability of their world is many times asserted. It succumbs to attack from without, as in the invasion of a band of city-gallants who piratically carry Chloe away for a while, and to attack from within: the repellent Gnathon forces his attentions upon Daphnis, and Chloe is attacked by the lustful Dorcon dressed in animal skins. Neither town nor country is awarded the palm, but perhaps the former derives a slight advantage from the fact that when the lovers are able to be so in fact, it is because Daphnis has finally been initiated into the mysteries of sexual pairing by a townswoman – of course it would be a townswoman. It is Longus's humorous way of saying that there is an art even in 'natural' functions and that nature, though she gives much, does not give all. The novel is astonishing for the equilibrium it maintains between the freshness and beauty of the pastoral world and the sense of its fragility and finally of its insufficiency. Nostalgia and wisdom go hand in hand, and the fusion of the two produces a marvellous good humour that lightens from every page.

Like the pastoral of rural life, whose essential characteristic is that it is written at a distance from the country and from a sophisticated point of view, the pastoral of childhood requires the adult perspective. Where poets in the early tradition generally initiated their careers with a set of Arcadian pastorals, the novelist who has succeeded him is generally wont to initiate his career with a story, either openly autobiographical or very thinly fictionalized, of childhood. Distant time has succeeded distant place as the great focus of pastoral interest, and the golden pastures of Arcadia have yielded to the golden time of childhood.

This emphasis on childhood and adolescence in our literature is sometimes not recognized, especially by the young, as the comparative novelty it is. Before Rousseau and the Romantic poets, only Henry Vaughan (and then in another context entirely) appears to be at all aware of the child as other than an embryonic adult. Ambrose Phillips, of course, won a reputation from Pope as a fool for his pastorals, but he had won it earlier by his sentimental poems on childhood, along with the epithet 'Namby-Pamby'. The emphasis on childhood is essentially a Romantic innovation based on the notion that the clear natural vision of the child is somehow superior to that of the man. It is an endearing idea, but we must take it on faith that it is truly so, for the innocence attributed to the child may be only the projection of the author's imaginings about that earlier state of life, and they are bound to be coloured by his experience and by his nostalgia. As shepherds do not write pastoral poetry, children do not write in praise of childhood. When we are presented with this wonderful phenomenon of the child wiser and more innocent than the man – we may use Wordsworth's *Prelude* as an example that unites the pastoral of rural life with the pastoral of childhood – it becomes a matter of real difficulty to disentangle the art of the adult author from the supposed naturalness of the child of whom he writes. In a very real sense, the Romantics discovered, not really the child himself, but a way of writing about him. Previous to Wordsworth, the accepted way to write about children was to treat them with a kind of gentle irony, a way that captured their fresh innocence, but also captured its fragility. One thinks immediately of Longus's novel, and in poetry, of Herrick, of Marvell and Matthew Prior. The Romantic innovation consisted in treating them with a sublimity of feeling that reflected the sublimity of their being: the same thing, it seems clear, occurred in the treatment of the shepherd.

Our novelists appear to have developed both ways of writing about children, lessening the sense of sublimity but preserving the sense of relative innocence in the one case, and preserving the sense of vulnerability and extending it into a real capacity for evil in the other case. There is a kind of Pelagian or Rousseauistic vision in the one, an Augustinian vision in the other. The two main forms our modern pastorals of innocence take, city and country pastorals of childhood, result in either naturalistic idylls in a rural setting or memoirs of a terrifying urban development of which the discovery of a sense of evil is the central focus. The field is vast, and we can choose only a few illustrative instances.

Thomas Wolfe's *Look Homeward, Angel*, Richard Llewellyn's *How Green Was My Valley*, Laurie Lee's *Cider with Rosie* may all stand as examples of the country pastoral of childhood. Here the life of the child, lived in some idyllic setting in the proximate past – South Carolina, Wales, the Cotswold Hills – is a generally ecstatic one of golden visions; it is not perfect, certainly, but it preserves some distant gleams of the golden age that irradiate their surroundings. What sexuality there is in these novels – and it is a ground-note in all of them as setting the boundary between childhood and maturity – is customarily voluptuous and pagan. The image that comes to mind for all of them is of a discovery of love on an idle summer afternoon in which all the blind strivings of youth to secret knowledge appear in sharper focus. The thirtieth chapter in the novels of both Wolfe and Llewellyn might have been headed as Laurie Lee headed his chapter on the entrance into sexual experience, 'First Bite at the Apple'. The Fall in the garden is repeated in all three, and the picture that springs to mind for all of them is that of the sensual Rosie stuffing her young swain's shoes with flowers as they lie for a long moment afterwards under the hay-rick in the summer heat. All the myths of hedonistic and wanton innocence in the golden age have been transferred from the shepherd to the child or young adolescent. Yet the entrance into sexual life represents a move into a world of experience, and sometimes there is a vivid sense of the awakening of a sense of sin as old as man, though it is merely glanced at and drowned in the rapture of the moment. This is Wolfe, aware of a disappointment to come and of the fact that he has snatched an apple from a Hesperian garden guarded by a dragon:

> They clung together in the bright moment of wonder, there on the magic island, where the world was quiet, believing all they said. And who shall say – whatever disenchantment follows – that we ever forget magic, or that we can ever betray, on this leaden earth, the apple-tree, the singing, and the gold?

And this is Llewellyn, as explicit as Lee in his recall of an old Fall and as uncaring:

> Then the tight-drawn branch is weak, for the string has sung its song, and breath comes back to empty lungs and a trembling to the limbs. Your eyes see plainly. The trees are green, just the same as they were. No change has come. No bolts of fire. No angels with a

flaming sword. Yet this it was that left the Garden to weeds. I had eaten of the Tree. Eve was still warm under me. Yet still no bolt, no fire, no swords. Only the song of a thrush, and the smell of green, and the peace of the mountain-side.

The experience of sex separates the child from the man; Lee's terse 'I was never the same again' might be a general motto for all.

The naturalness with which these boys enter upon their sexual lives reflects the naturalness of their surroundings: the natural world is the scene and the benign witness of their rapture. The torment of childhood plays little part in these naturalistic idylls, but it is in the foreground of the city pastorals, which more often than not portray the child as the victim of the adult world of experience whose innocence is asserted even as he struggles blindly to enter that world. One thinks immediately of the Stephen Dedalus of Joyce and his innocent quest for Dublin whores, of J. D. Salinger's innocent sophisticate Holden Caulfield in his amusing encounters with New York prostitutes in shady hotels, of the immigrant child David Schearl's desperate fumblings towards a forbidden knowledge in tenement rooms in Henry Roth's grim and horrific but tremendously powerful *Call It Sleep*. And one thinks too, inevitably, of Philip Roth's most recent novel, *Portnoy's Complaint*, where the sexual instinct turns in upon itself and achieves a comic explosion of desperately innocent wantonness. As I write, I notice that there has just been published a book entitled *The True Adventures of Huckleberry Finn*, by John Seelye, which is a rewriting of Mark Twain's classic pastoral of youth, and which apparently manages to infuse into it all those things which the modern view of childhood conceives to be missing in its pages, notably sex and the repeal of illusions about limitless horizons: there is no 'lighting out' for the Territory here. The city pastoral is extending a long reach.

Whether modern psychology or simple experience has taught us better, we are no longer accustomed to see childhood as a rapturous and lyrical existence, and we are probably in a post-Arcadian phase of the pastoral of childhood. In certain contemporary novels we find prevailing not only an unsentimental but a distinctly Augustinian view of human nature that sees the child as quite literally the father of the man in respect of his tendency to evil. These novels put no emphasis on sexuality whatever; the inclination to evil is demonstrated through a propensity to violence and cunning and secretiveness. Richard Hughes's *A High Wind in Jamaica* is an example. Two others are Ferenc Molnar's *The Boys on Paul Street* and William Golding's *Lord of the Flies*. With these, of course, we have passed into allegory: in Molnar, the street-games of a group of boys become a projection of the territorial ambitions leading to war which have immemorially racked the progress of the race; in Golding, the crash of a plane deposits a group of boys upon an island of primitive beauty which becomes the scene of primitive blood-lust on one hand and of primitive innocence on the other. The novel shatters all the romantic conceptions about childhood and natural goodness and the holiness of the heart's affections. Nor is it a paean to the world of Art, for the youths who revert to savagery are themselves the inheritors of all of the gains that mankind has made so painfully after the first expulsion from the garden. In its refusal to find an easy solution in either Nature or Art, its attribution of evil to the individual and not to surroundings, the novel is truly and seriously pastoral in its movement.

6
Conclusion

What will succeed to child-cult as a version of pastoral, no one has yet told us, but the pace of modern life is accelerating so greatly that the pace of literature is bound to be affected as well. If the child has half as long a literary life as the shepherd, he will be remarkable. Publishers continue, however, almost daily to announce new novels, new memoirs of childhood, and there is no fear that the fashion will end, or that one version of pastoral at least will not be with us for some time to come. Considering the spoliation of nature which our age is accomplishing to such an extent that the capacity of the life processes to continue in our time are daily being questioned, it is fortunate, perhaps, that the child has taken over the role of the shepherd. Residing in a definite landscape, the shepherd needed an external world of lovely fresh nature in which to appear; residing only in time, the child can survive as an emblem of innocence without it. As the evidence of a deep-rooted instinct for perfection, pastoral will survive even in this age of unthought-of horrors, perhaps flourish because of it. The descent to an age of plastic was something not contemplated by the ancients, who stopped at iron.

Bibliography

BARBER, C. L., 'The Alliance of Seriousness and Levity in *As You Like It*', in *Shakespeare's Festive Comedy*, Princeton, 1959.
A major consideration of the play.

BUXTON, JOHN, 'Sidney: The Countess of Pembroke's *Arcadia*', in *Elizabethan Taste*, London, 1963.
A good treatment of what the period saw in the work.

BUXTON, JOHN, 'Michael Drayton', in *A Tradition of Poetry*, London, 1967.
An appreciation of Drayton as life-long pastoralist.

CHAMBERS, E. K., *English Pastorals*, London, 1895.
An anthology with a valuable brief introduction.

CHENEY, DONALD, *Spenser's Image of Nature: Wild Man and Shepherd in The Faerie Queene*, New Haven, 1966.
An especially good chapter on Book VI.

CONGLETON, J. E., *Theories of Pastoral Poetry in England, 1684–1798*, Gainesville, Florida, 1952.
A good survey of French and English attitudes to pastoral in the age of its degeneracy.

CORY, HERBERT E., 'The Golden Age of the Spenserian Pastoral', *PMLA*, XXV (1910), pp. 241–67.
An early and still valid survey of the pastoralists who followed Spenser, particularly Greene, Drayton, Browne, and Fletcher.

CURTIUS, E. R., *European Literature in the Latin Middle Ages*, tr. Willard Trask, New York, 1953.
To be consulted for its discussion of the *locus amoenus*.

DIPPLE, ELIZABETH, 'Harmony and Pastoral in the *Old Arcadia*', *ELH*, XXV (1968), pp. 309–28.

This and the following monograph are new and intriguing expositions of the Neoplatonic element in Sidney.

DIPPLE, ELIZABETH, 'The "Fore Conceit" of Sidney's Eclogues', in *Literary Monographs*, ed. Eric Rothstein and Thomas K. Dunseath, Madison, 1967.

EMPSON, WILLIAM, *Some Versions of Pastoral*, London, 1950.

A difficult and erratic but always exciting book that more than any other has extended the use of the term.

GIAMATTI, A. BARTLETT, *The Earthly Paradise and the Renaissance Epic*, Princeton, 1966.

A fine comparative study of the *locus amoenus* as the arena for love.

GOW, A. S. F., *The Greek Bucolic Poets*, Cambridge, 1953.

Some very readable translations of Theocritus, Bion and Moschus, with a valuable introduction, especially for the poems of the first.

GREENLAW, E., 'Shakespeare's Pastorals', *Studies in Philology*, XIII (1916), pp. 122–54.

An extensive study of Shakespeare's pastoral plays against the background of the pastoral romances.

GREG, W. W., *Pastoral Poetry and Pastoral Drama*, London, 1906.

The standard source for the older pastoral; indispensable.

HAMILTON, A. C., 'The Argument of Spenser's *Shepheardes Calender*', *ELH*, XXIII (1956), pp. 171–82.

One of the best modern readings.

HANFORD, J. H., 'The Pastoral Elegy and Milton's *Lycidas*', *PMLA*, XXV (1910), pp. 403–47.

Still the standard source of the background in Greek elegy of Milton's poem.

HENINGER, S. K., JR., 'The Renaissance Perversion of Pastoral', *Journal of the History of Ideas*, XXII (1961), pp. 254–61.

Represents the frequent antagonism to all pastoral not essentially lyric and sees the introduction of moral, satiric and sentimental elements into the form as essentially a perversion of its nature.

HARRISON, T. P., and LEON, H. J., *The Pastoral Elegy*, Austin, Texas, 1939.

The best anthology with some fine translations.

JONES, W. P., *The Pastourelle*, Oxford, 1931.

A good study of the origins and permutations of the form.

KALSTONE, DAVID, *Sidney's Poetry*, Cambridge, Mass., 1965.

Some splendid commentary on Sannazaro and Sidney as Arcadians in the first three chapters.

KENNEDY, JUDITH M., *A Critical Edition of Yong's Translation of George of Montemayor's Diana and Gil Polo's Enamoured Diana*, Oxford, 1968.

An edition of one of the most famous pastoral-chivalric romances of the sixteenth century, preceded by a good introduction.

KERMODE, FRANK, ed., *The Tempest*, Arden edition, London, 1954, new ed. 1958.

The introduction contains the best and fullest exposition of the Nature-Art antithesis; a classic and essential work.

KERMODE, FRANK, ed., *English Pastoral Poetry from the Beginnings to Marvell*, London, 1952.

A fine anthology with a very informative introduction.

LEVIN, HARRY, *The Myth of the Golden Age in the Renaissance*, Bloomington, 1969.

An extensive survey of the idea in its literary and artistic manifestations.

LINCOLN, ELEANOR TERRY, ed., *Pastoral and Romance: Modern Essays in Criticism*, Prentice-Hall Paperbacks, New Jersey, 1969.

A very useful work: contains well-chosen excerpts from modern critical writing on pastoral.

LYNEN, JOHN F., *The Pastoral Art of Robert Frost*, Yale Paperbacks, New Haven, 1960.

The best study of Frost as pastoralist in the modern sense of the term; a splendid chapter on 'New Hampshire as Arcadia'.

MACK, MAYNARD, *The Garden and the City*, Toronto, 1969.

A superbly written and illustrated study of Pope in retirement at Twickenham, consciously recreating a private Arcadia of the spirit.

MARX, LEO, *The Machine in the Garden: Technology and the Pastoral Ideal in America*, Oxford Galaxy, New York, 1967.

The classic study of the American Arcadian ideal and the first movements towards its destruction.

MCLANE, PAUL E., *Spenser's Shepheardes Calender: A Study in Elizabethan Allegory*, Notre Dame, 1961.

A full study of the historical background, resulting in an identification of Spenser's cast of shepherds with which not everyone will be in agreement, but which is suggestive nevertheless.

NASH, RALPH, tr., *Jacopo Sannazaro's Arcadia and Piscatorial Eclogues*, Detroit, 1966.

The first translation into English of both works; contains a brief and illuminating introduction.

PATRIDES, C. A., ed., *Milton's Lycidas: The Tradition and the Poem*, New York, 1961.

Collects the major critical writings on the poem; the interpretation by Rosemond Tuve is especially worthwhile. A very useful guide.

POGGIOLI, RENATO, 'The Oaten Flute', *Harvard Library Bulletin*, XI (1957), pp. 147–84.

Before his untimely death the author was planning to collect this and the following articles into a work on pastoral. I understand that Harvard University Press is currently preparing the work, to be published under the title *The Oaten Flute: A Study of Pastoral Poetry and the Bucolic Ideal*. This article is notable for the distinction it makes between the pastoral of happiness and the pastoral of innocence.

POGGIOLI, RENATO, 'The Pastoral of the Self', *Daedalus*, LXXXVIII (1959), pp. 686–99.
A superb study of the pastoral withdrawal for pure cultivation of the self, drawing upon Cervantes and upon Marvell's 'The Garden' for illustration.

POGGIOLO, RENATO, 'Naboth's Vineyard or the Pastoral View of the Social Order', *Journal of the History of Ideas*, XXIV (1963), pp. 3–24.
A brilliant exposition of the pastoral idea of justice.

ROSENMEYER, THOMAS G., *The Green Cabinet: Theocritus and the European Pastoral Lyric*, Berkeley, 1969.
A study which ranges over the entire field, taking the poems of Theocritus as a norm for pastoral.

SMITH, HALLETT, *Elizabethan Poetry*, Cambridge, Mass., 1952.
Contains well-balanced discussions on Elizabethan poetry divided into genres; two fine introductory chapters on pastoral and epic.

SNELL, BRUNO, *The Discovery of the Mind: the Greek Origins of European Thought*, Harper Torchbooks, New York, 1960.
The last chapter contains what is probably the best single piece of criticism on Virgil's *Eclogues* yet written.

STATON, WALTER F., JR., and SIMEONE, WALTER E., eds. *A Critical Edition of Sir Richard Fanshawe's 1647 Translation of Giovanni Battista Guarini's Il Pastor Fido*, Oxford, 1964.
Contains some valuable remarks on the pastoral drama in its introduction.

TAYLER, EDWARD WILLIAM, *Nature and Art in Renaissance Literature*, New York, 1964.
A clearly-written and well-planned survey of classical, medieval, and Renaissance treatments of the two ideas.

TINKER, C. B., *Nature's Simple Plan*, Princeton, 1922.

A delightful chapter on the 'natural' poets of the eighteenth century.

TOLIVER, HAROLD E., *Marvell's Ironic Vision*, New Haven, 1965.

A controversial but illuminating reading of Marvell; the chapter 'Pastoral and Reconciliation with History' contains some interesting ideas.

WALLACE, JOHN M., 'Milton's *Arcades*', *Journal of English and Germanic Philology*, LVIII (1959), pp. 627–36. Reprinted in *Milton: Modern Essays in Criticism*, ed. Arthur E. Barker, Oxford Galaxy, New York, 1965.

WILLIAMS, KATHLEEN, *Spenser's Faerie Queene: The World of Glass*, London, 1966.

Contains a sensitive and beautifully-written chapter on the pastoral Book VI.

Index

DATE DUE
